CHARACTER AND CONTEXT

Program in Judaic Studies
Brown University
BROWN JUDAIC STUDIES
Edited by
Jacob Neusner,
Wendell S. Dietrich, Ernest S. Frerichs,
Alan Zuckerman

Project Editors (Project)

David Blumenthal, Emory University (Approaches to Medieval Judaism)
Lenn Evan Goodman, University of Hawaii (Studies in Medieval Judaism)
William Scott Green, University of Rochester (Approaches to Ancient Judaism)
Marc L. Raphael, Ohio State University (Approaches to Judaism in Modern Times)
Jonathan Z. Smith, University of Chicago (Studia Philonica)

Number 45

CHARACTER AND CONTEXT
Studies in the Fiction
of Abramovitsh, Brenner, and Agnon

by
Jeffrey Fleck

CHARACTER AND CONTEXT
Studies in the Fiction of Abramovitsh, Brenner, and Agnon

by
Jeffrey Fleck

Scholars Press
Chico, California

CHARACTER AND CONTEXT
Studies in the Fiction
of Abramovitsh, Brenner, and Agnon

by
Jeffrey Fleck

© 1984
Brown University

Publication of this book has been made possible
in part by a gift from
THE SIMON FUND FOR JUDAIC STUDIES
AT
BROWN UNIVERSITY

Library of Congress Cataloging in Publication Data
Fleck, Jeffrey.
　Character and context.

　(Brown Judaic studies ; 45)
　Bibliography: p.
　Includes index.
　1. Hebrew fiction—History and criticism—Addresses, essays, lectures. 2. Mendele Mokher Sefarim, 1835-1917. Sefer ha-kabtsanim. 3. Brenner, Joseph Hayyim, 1881-1921— Criticism and interpretation. 4. Agnon, Shmuel Yosef, 1888-1970. Temol shilshom. I. Title. III. Series: Brown Judaic Studies ; no. 45.
PJ5029.F4　1984　　892.4'35'09　　　　83-9068
ISBN 0-89130-643-X

Printed in the United States of America
on acid-free paper

To My Mother and Father

WITHDRAWN

HARVARD LIBRARY

WITHDRAWN

TABLE OF CONTENTS

Preface 1

Chapter One: Modern Hebrew Literature in Context 3

Chapter Two: Is There a Person in the Text? 21

Chapter Three: Mendele in Pieces: S.Y. Abramovitsh's <u>The Beggars' Book</u> 43

Chapter Four: The Drama of Narration: Y.H. Brenner's <u>In Winter</u> 59

Chapter Five: Narrative as Psychological Drama: Y.H. Brenner's
<u>Breakdown and Bereavement</u> 73

Chapter Six: Man and Dog in S.Y. Agnon's <u>Only Yesterday</u> 87

Chapter Seven: Conclusion 103

Notes 109

Works Consulted 119

Index 125

PREFACE

This work has a double focus. First, it is a study of four novels by three of the best novelists that modern Hebrew literature has produced, S.Y. Abramovitsh (1835-1917), commonly known by his nom de plume, Mendele Mokher Sefarim, Y.H. Brenner (1881-1921), and S.Y. Agnon (1888-1970). Since neither the works of these authors (with the possible exception of Agnon) nor the literary and cultural environments in which they worked are familiar to most English readers, I treat these matters at some length in Chapter One, "Modern Hebrew Literature in Context." Secondly, this work considers a theoretical issue in narrative discourse which, in spite of the revival of formalist and theoretical approaches to fiction of the last two decades, has generally been treated tangentially or not at all. The issue is the nature and function of characters in narrative discourse and, more specifically, their relation to the narrative structures in which they appear. Thus, the "context" in the title does not refer to the historical or social factors that may determine, to one degree or another, the kind of characters that appear in a novel of a particular period, but rather the needs and requirements of a particular genre, in this case the novel, and the manner in which those needs and requirements determine the nature of what we refer to as fictional characters. In Chapter Two, "Is There a Person in the Text?," I analyze the strengths and weaknesses of Structuralist and Semiotic approaches to this question from the Russian Formalists to Roland Barthes and the Israeli semiotician, Benjamin Hrushovski.

These two foci come together in the analyses of the novels themselves. No attempt, however, is made to systematically apply any of the theories or interpretive strategies discussed in Chapter Two. As my account of those theories and strategies indicates, most of them contain serious limitations with regard to the question of characters in fiction. Indeed, if the ability to account for the central place characters have in our experience of reading fiction is any criterion, then most of those "narratologies" are simply failures. But it is not my intention to use my analyses of the novels simply as occasions to point out, tediously and repetitively, those limitations and failures. Rather, I propose to apply those perspectives and insights generated by structural and semiotic approaches to fiction that offer, in my view, a basis for doing what the Structuralists and Semioticians themselves have, for a variety of reasons, failed to do. Thus, my analyses of the novels center upon the protagonist as a functioning unit in the overall narrative structure (rather than, for example, as a more or less convincing mimesis) and I attempt to make explicit in each case the relationship between the protagonist (as function) and the other formal and thematic patterns that constitute that structure. In the Conclusion, I provide an abstract summary of the strategies I have applied to the analysis of the novels and briefly consider what a broader application of those strategies might mean for the study of a literary tradition that is characterized by swift transformations and radical discontinuities.

This work is a revised version of my Ph.D. dissertation written for the Department of Comparative Literature at the University of California, Berkeley. Frederick Crews of the Department of English at Berkeley and Meir Sternberg of Tel Aviv University read the dissertation in various stages of its development. I would like to thank them once again for their perceptive comments and suggestions. Ziva ben Porath of Tel Aviv University read an early chapter of the dissertation while serving as Visiting Professor of Comparative Literature at Berkeley. Her comments were both provocative and encouraging. A long conversation with Benjamin Hrushovski, while he was serving as Visiting Professor of Comparative Literature at Berkeley, provided me with some key ideas and insights that literally changed the course of my work. I am particularly grateful to Robert Alter, my graduate advisor and chairman of my dissertation committee, whose teaching and scholarly example provided an ideal atmosphere for my literary education at Berkeley.

Professor Marc Raphael, a member of the editorial board of Brown Judaic Studies, read my dissertation during a particularly trying period of my career and was the first to suggest I publish it in the series. Alan Mintz of the University of Maryland, editor of the series for Hebrew Literature, provided detailed and substantive comments on the entire manuscript. I thank them both for their time and consideration. Some of the funds for publication of the manuscript were provided by the Melton Center for Jewish Studies of Columbus, Ohio.

I would like to extend special thanks to the members of the Program in Judaic Studies of Brown University, Ernest S. Frerichs, co-director, Wendell S. Dietrich, Sidney Goldstein, David Hirsch, David Sorkin, and Alan Zuckerman, for their collegial friendship and support, and particularly to Jacob Neusner, co-director of the Program, without whose encouragement this book would not have come to press.

Chapter Three, parts of Chapter Four, and Chapter Six appeared previously in slightly different forms in the journals Prooftexts, AJS Review, and Hebrew Annual Review, respectively. I thank the editors for permission to use them here.

Finally, I wish to thank my wife, Deborah Steinhardt, whose perceptive and informed comments helped me in working out some of the central issues treated in this work.

Jeffrey Fleck

Program in Judaic Studies
Brown University
May 6, 1984

CHAPTER ONE

Modern Hebrew Literature in Context

Modern Hebrew literature did not evolve naturally or inevitably out of pre-modern secular literary tradition. It was initiated by an act of will of a small group of German Jews toward the end of the 18th century in a literary vacuum and for a readership that did not exist. Lacking both a past to define itself against and a body of readerly expectations to fulfill or frustrate, the literature's development during its first hundred years was both swift and erratic. Linguistic and stylistic breakthroughs and thematic innovations which in more normal circumstances might have been a matter of centuries emerged and passed from the scene within a single generation. What was considered bold and daring by one generation of writers became obsolete and archaic in the eyes of the next. Even works by contemporaries often diverged so radically in form or thematic focus that they seem to come from different centuries. Closet dramas in verse and romantic lyrics, epic poems, historical romances, and realistic novels of contemporary life appeared simultaneously or in close succession. Literary schools and movements proliferated and overlapped so that, by the beginning of the 20th century, there were Hebrew writers of the same or adjacent generations who could be associated with classicism, romanticism, neo-romanticism, social realism, naturalism, psychological fiction, literary engagement, and "art for art's sake."

The German Jews who initiated this process were also among the founders of the Haskalah, the Jewish Enlightenment movement which would, in the course of the 19th century, along with the new literature, spread eastward until it reached its fullest expression in the second half of the century in the Russian Pale of Settlement. The goal of these early maskilim was nothing less than the complete transformation of Jewish society and culture according to the ideology and values of the German Aufklaerung, a process which, in their eyes, would bring the Jews out of the darkness of their medieval existence into the clear light of the increasingly secular modern world. Since they considered Yiddish to be an unsuitable medium for their program of reason and "good taste," they turned to Hebrew as a means of reaching the more educated segments of traditional Jewish society. For the maskilim, Hebrew, unlike Yiddish, was a "pure" language and, thanks to the models provided by the Hebrew Scriptures, uniquely suited for "sublime" expression. Indeed, they viewed the language itself as a source of intellectual and spiritual improvement and often wrote enthusiastically of its beauty and power. One of the earliest Haskalah societies, which was responsible for the publication of the first modern Hebrew periodical, called itself "Friends of the Hebrew Language." The early maskils' attempts at "belles-lettres" -- epic poems, closet dramas, proverbs, maxims and fables -- were, however, quite stiff and imitative and dominated by an overt and often crude didacticism. It is not altogether surprising, then, that as one of the main goals of the Haskalah was achieved -- the adoption by Jews of the language of the land -- Hebrew was largely abandoned by the next generation of German maskilim.

Hebrew literature gained new life when the Haskalah, having left its mark in Galicia, began to take root in the Pale of Settlement. But here, too, in spite of a deeper commitment to Hebrew on the part of many of the Russian maskilim, the literature remained largely subservient to the Haskalah message. While the historical romances of Abraham Mapu and the novels of contemporary Jewish life in the Pale of Settlement of Peretz Smolenskin and Reuben Asher Braudes are in many ways superior to earlier maskilic works written in Hebrew, the awkward manner in which the last two authors attempted to combine flamboyantly melodramatic plots culled from French romantic fiction with their messages of educational reform and social improvement, along with the general crudeness of their narrative technique, prevented them from producing any works of literary distinction.

The literary achievement of the novelists of the Russian Haskalah, however, was not only limited by their preoccupation with their message. The very choice of Hebrew as a modern, tendentiously secular literary medium was itself a source of enormous difficulties. Hebrew had enjoyed an active life as a written language throughout the Middle Ages, but it had not been employed as a spoken language in everyday life since the end of the second century. Moreover, as leshon hakodesh (the holy tongue), its writing had been largely confined to specifically religious genres -- liturgical poetry, biblical exegesis, talmudic commentary, codes of religious law, ethical, philosophical, and mystical speculation -- so that while the language developed and expanded its expressive capabilities, it did so in a relatively limited sphere. The medieval poets of the Spanish School (950-1150), who borrowed both their rules of prosody and their secular motifs from Arabic models, represent the most significant exception to the general dominance of religious genres in Hebrew letters of the Middle Ages. They were, however, quite conservative in matters of language and prided themselves in their biblical "purism."

In any event, the writers of the Haskalah avoided the Hebrew that emerged out of the Middle Ages since, for them, it was closely associated with the rabbinic tradition whose insularity and obscurantism were the chief targets of their ridicule. Like the Hebrew poets of the Spanish School, the maskilim chose to write in biblical Hebrew, which in their eyes was purer and more sublime than the Hebrew of the rabbis. As a result, the novelists who set their works in contemporary Jewish society in the Pale ended up writing novels in a language not only not spoken by anyone in that society, but one which virtually nobody had spoken for nearly two millenia.

The difficulties that such a situation creates for the novel, a genre in which realistic dialogue plays such an important role, can be illustrated by the experience of the author of the first Hebrew novel (more properly, a historical romance), Avraham Mapu. Mapu's first work, The Love of Zion (1853), is set in the Land of Israel during the period of Isaiah and involves a series of interlocking melodramatic plots and love intrigues drawn from the Italian pastoral tradition which reached Mapu through the Hebrew allegorical dramas of Moshe Haim Luzzato (1707-1746). The fact that the novel is written in a nearly pure biblical Hebrew, then, is not only justified by the novel's period and setting, it serves to reinforce the "biblical" atmosphere that Mapu wanted to evoke. (A century later, the Israeli novelist Moshe Shamir would write his historical novel of the Second Temple period, King of Flesh and Blood, in mishnaic Hebrew in order to achieve a similar effect.) Moreover, the highly conventional and stylized nature of the drama along with its declamatory dialogues and set speeches lent themselves well to a Hebrew far removed from the patterns of everyday speech. In his second novel, The Hypocrite (first part, 1858; complete edition, posthumously in 1869), however, Mapu attempted to write of contemporary life in the Russian Pale, and here the use of biblical Hebrew became far more problematic. Mapu's efforts to create an illusion of realism in the speech of his characters by introducing elements of mishnaic Hebrew into the dialogues (while the narrative exposition remained largely biblical) only served to emphasize the artificiality of his language and the wide gap between his novel and the Yiddish-speaking environment he wanted to describe.[1]

Even after Hebrew literature overcame the thematic limitations of the Haskalah and began, in the last decades of the 19th century, to produce writers and works of some stature, it could still be characterized as a "literature in a vacuum."[2] Its readership, which had never been very large, was diminishing rapidly. The main source of potential readers, the emerging youthful intelligentsia, turned increasingly to Russian political and social affairs, either through direct participation in Russian revolutionary movements, or through the Yiddish socialist movement. Moreover, the geographical base of the literature was deteriorating as writers and readers alike joined the Jewish flight from Russia which, by the turn of the century, had reached massive proportions. Odessa and Warsaw, the two major centers of Hebrew literary activity in the 1880's and 1890's, had become by the beginning of the 20th century no more than way stations for the younger writers on their way to the West. Though generally sympathetic to Zionism, few of the writers who had begun their literary careers in Russia were attracted to the limited and provincial cultural atmosphere of the new Jewish settlement in Palestine. Thus, its writers wandering between the cultural centers of Europe and, in a few cases, America, Hebrew literature became a literature of émigrés. Finally, the problem of language persisted. Having rejected the biblical pastiche of the Haskalah, Hebrew novelists were faced with the task of inventing a literary idiom that could serve the needs of their increasingly realistic and psychologically sophisticated fiction. With the very ability among young Jews to read Hebrew on the decline, and themselves scattered between Russia, Europe, America and Palestine, Hebrew writers at the turn of the century not only had to maintain their faith in a revived Hebrew language, they had to guess, as it were, what such a language would look and sound like.[3]

Hebrew writers were hardly unaware of these circumstances. Indeed, they often wondered if they were really the vanguard of national and cultural revival, as they often claimed, or simply writing the closing chapter of a noble but ultimately doomed experiment. Their literature is one of extreme shifts in outlook and mood. Bitterly pessimistic self-appraisal often comes at the heels of bold assertions of vitality. The literature itself is often described as a dead or dying enterprise with only slim chances of survival. To the protagonist of M.Z. Feierberg's influential novel, <u>Whither</u> (1899), Hebrew literature is like "a bucketful of fish in rancid water."

> They first darted this way and that, they twisted and squirmed and poked their heads above water to look for the air that they lacked... so Hebrew literature twisted and squirmed too...[4]

Even as Hebrew writers feverishly pursued their task of reconstruction and innovation, often producing works of genuine artistic merit, death and decay -- whether of the crumbling world of traditional Jewish society or the uprooted youth in search of a new spiritual home -- became one of their obsessive themes.

The material and cultural circumstances responsible for much of the pessimism and gloom that pervades many of the works written during this period also instilled a sense of urgency in those who remained committed to Hebrew literature. The decades surrounding the turn of the century were vital and productive ones for Hebrew literature and the artistic accomplishments of its best writers -- Bialik and Tchernichowsky in poetry; Abramovitsh, Peretz, Brenner, Gnessin, Shofman in prose -- has not been matched in subsequent periods. In spite of limited funds, dwindling readership, and the Russian censors, Hebrew publishing houses and the periodicals in which the works of these and scores of other writers appeared remained active up to the outbreak of the Bolshevik Revolution, and some, like Bialik's and Rawnitzki's Moriah, reemerged in Mandatory Palestine under different names. The proliferation of Hebrew periodicals in this period reflects the variety of literary ideologies and schools that sprung up around the most influential writers of the day. The stylistic classicism and utilitarian ethic of Ahad Ha-Am and his followers, the neo-romanticism of Y.L. Peretz, the naturalism of Ben-Avigdor, the psychological fiction and literary experimentation of the "younger generation," as well as the extensive translation projects of David Frishman, all competed for the attention of the ever diminishing ranks of Hebrew readers.

* * *

The literary careers of S.Y. Abramovitsh (1835-1917), Y.H. Brenner (1881-1921), and S.Y. Agnon (1888-1970) amply illustrate the linguistic, stylistic, thematic and ideological turmoil that characterized modern Hebrew literature from its very inception and which became particularly intense at the turn of the century. For while they represent three distinct literary generations and, as we shall see, diverged in whole or part on almost every significant literary question, they were also contemporaries and each published important works in the first two decades of the 20th century. During these years, Abramovitsh continued to write original works in Yiddish, revised and added significant portions to earlier works, and prepared the final Hebrew versions of his major novels. The publication between 1909 and 1912 of the three-volume "Jubilee Edition" of his collected Hebrew works, which included the final version of <u>The Beggars' Book</u>, was a major literary event of the period. Brenner published his first short story in 1900, and this was followed in quick succession by a collection of short stories (1900), and the novellas In Winter (1903), Beside the Point (1904), One Year (1908), Between Water and Water (1910), and From Here and There (1911). The complete edition of his last work, the novel Breakdown and Bereavement, appeared in 1920. While still in his teens in Galicia, Agnon published poetry, short stories, and essays in Yiddish and Hebrew. His first important Hebrew short story, "Agunot," was published in Jaffa in 1908, and by 1920 he had published such significant early works as "And the Crooked Shall Become Straight," "The Banished One," the Polish "Legends," and "The Hill of Sand."

The links between the three writers, however, go far beyond chronological coincidence. Brenner, for example, was thoroughly familiar with Abramovitsh's works, both in Yiddish and Hebrew, and greatly admired them, a stance that was not always shared by others among the "younger generation" of writers for whom Brenner often served as spokesman. As early as 1904 Brenner had lectured on Abramovitsh in London[5] and his essay devoted to the "Jubilee Edition," "Self Evaluation in the Three Volumes," has become a classic of Hebrew literary criticism. In this essay, Brenner admitted that Abramovitsh did not present deep or complex psychological portraits -- "In the individualization of his heroes, as people would say today, Mendele the story teller does not perform wonders..."[6] -- but he was the first Hebrew writer, according to Brenner, to evoke a true picture of Jewish life in the traditional community and the first, moreover, to do so in the critical spirit of national "self-evaluation." Abramovitsh's artistry sprung from the world in which he lived (at least in the early years of his life) and of which he wrote, and while the younger writers had to explore new stylistic and thematic territories, he remained for Brenner "the first artist in our modern literature."

Brenner also had great admiration for the artistic qualities of Agnon's work, although in this case he was dealing not with the final expression of a mature artist but with the first efforts of a younger contemporary. Arguing the merits, in spite of its narrow "platform," of the Hebrew journal, Ha'omer, Brenner singled out Agnon's "Agunot" as a work of great originality that made a powerful impression, gave "great artistic pleasure," and, indeed, "rises above everything that is usually published among us."[7] In 1912, while he was living in Jerusalem, Brenner saw to the publication of Agnon's first book, an edition of "And The Crooked Shall Become Straight," which had appeared earlier that year in Hapo'el hatsa'ir. In the years that followed, Brenner would have occasion to publicly criticize the romantic and sentimental tendencies in Agnon's early works, but this criticism was always tempered by his admiration for the lyrical power of Agnon's prose.[8] Writing in 1920 of "The Legend of the Scribe," he held up Agnon's work as proof of the poetic powers of the Hebrew language. "From now on we will not pale before those who harass us: there is no basis for Hebrew poetry... S.Y. Agnon is with us."[9]

Agnon had first met Brenner in Lemberg in 1908[10] on his way to Palestine. After Brenner's arrival in Jaffa a year later, the two developed a close personal relationship and, by Agnon's account, were nearly constant companions while they lived there.[11] The young and at that time relatively unknown Agnon was clearly influenced by Brenner's strictures against the romantic excesses of his early stories, and his reworkings of many of those stories for later editions bear the traces of that influence. But even at this early stage of his career, Agnon understood that, for all he could learn from Brenner, he still had to find his own voice. In his correspondence with Brenner he could on occasion display great artistic independence. Regarding the publication of "Miriam's Well," Agnon wrote to Brenner in 1909 that he was "sure that you will not add to my words and will not put more tears into my well..."[12] Years later, in an essay written on the occasion of the fortieth anniversary of Brenner's death, Agnon would characterize the difference between his and Brenner's artistic paths in this way:

> Brenner did not have an imagination. On completing the writing of a book, he exhausted in it the entire fruit of his observation of the world that happened to come under his view, that is, that reality in which he found himself and whose essence he extracted. Which is not the case for one who possesses imagination, and, it goes without saying, one who possesses vision, who, even as he works on one book, sees thirteen other books that he must write.[13]

For Agnon, who clearly considered himself in the second class of writers he describes, Brenner's work revealed both the powers and weaknesses of an art too closely bound to immediate experience.

Brenner's influence upon Agnon, in any event, went far beyond specifically literary concerns. For Agnon, as for many of his generation, Brenner was a hero of the spirit, an almost saintly figure who refused to bow under adversity:

> Besides the fact that Brenner was a great writer who wrote books that are still innovative, he stood up for our literature in its day of hardship and saved from his scant bread and published <u>Hame'orer</u> and <u>Revivim</u> and books by Shofman, Gnessin, and Orlov and also my first book... And every <u>pruta</u> that came into his hands from the booksellers he gave to the author and did not take a commission for himself. There are those who labor in order to make a living and those who labor in order to gain honor; Brenner labored for our writers and our literature, and everything he did he did gladly.[14]

Brenner's absolute commitment to Hebrew literature, at a time dominated by disorientation and self-doubt, and his ready willingness to sacrifice what little he had in order to promote the careers of worthy young writers, made him, in Agnon's eyes, more than a literary figure. Brenner embodied for Agnon the <u>halutz</u> ideal, that spirit of dedication and self-sacrifice that he found so attractive in the young Zionist idealists (as opposed to the ideologues) who went out to work the land. In his novel of the Second Aliyah, <u>Only Yesterday</u> (1945), Agnon presents a brief glimpse of Brenner at a coffee house in Jaffa that provides a striking contrast to the atmosphere of spiritual ennui and disillusionment that pervades much of the novel.[15]

Both Brenner and Agnon felt a strong attachment to the works of Abramovitsh, but each developed his art in ways the older writer could hardly have imagined. Brenner regarded Agnon's prose as proof of the poetic powers of the Hebrew language, but he distrusted Agnon's romantic and sentimental tendencies and what he considered his detachment from life. ("Even fictional stories," he once told him, "are not exempt from a bit of reality."[16]) Agnon considered Brenner an important innovator and spiritual example, but had to "overcome" his influence before his own voice and vision could emerge. Thus, while the literary careers of the three authors converged during the first two decades of the 20th century and the mutual influences between them were both ample and significant, it is, finally, the manner in which their work differs, both in underlying conception and narrative realization, that is the most striking aspect of their relationship.

* * *

Depending upon how you look at it, Abramovitsh's fiction represents the culmination of the literature of the Russian Haskalah or the beginning of a new period in which Hebrew literature, freed to a large degree from the didactic preoccupations of the Haskalah, came of age artistically. Abramovitsh's long and productive literary career does in fact span both periods, and while he remained a distinct voice in modern Hebrew literature, his development as an artist reflects the changes and developments that took place in the Jewish literary climate in Russia during the second half of the 19th and first decades of the 20th centuries.

Abramovitsh received a traditional Jewish education in the small town of Belorussia where he was born in 1835 and studied in various yeshivot in Lithuania after the death of his father in 1848. By his late teens, however, he was studying Russian, German, and Hebrew Haskalah literature under the tutelage of A.B. Gottlober, an influential maskil of the period, and by the age of twenty-two he had published his first Hebrew essay, "A Letter on Education," a typical maskilic tract calling for reform in Jewish educational practices. Abramovitsh's multi-volume work, Natural History (1862-1873), which draws freely upon books of popular science written in German, reflects the importance that the Haskalah placed upon instruction in the sciences, particularly the natural sciences. Abramovitsh's first Hebrew novel, Fathers and Sons (1868), is firmly grounded in the Haskalah tradition both in its overtly didactic intentions and in the biblical style of its language that is reminiscent of the Hebrew of Mapu's The Love of Zion.

It was, indeed, Abramovitsh's adherence to the Haskalah's utilitarian conception of art that led him, in the 1870's, to abandon Hebrew for his short stories and novels and turn instead to Yiddish, the first (and, in most cases, the only) language of the majority of Jews in Russia. Abramovitsh believed that his fiction, like his work on the natural sciences, could help improve the life of the Jews of Russia, but only if it could reach an audience larger than a handful of maskilim who, in any event, did not need to be convinced of the need for radical change in Jewish society. Thus, while he largely shared the maskilic distaste for Yiddish, at least at this stage of his career, he turned to it in order to find the proper audience for his fiction, even as he continued to publish essays on maskilic themes in Hebrew.[17] The choice of Yiddish had, of course, some obvious artistic advantages. Abramovitsh could now write of Jewish society in the Pale of Settlement in the language in which that society conducted its affairs, and he could adopt his prose to the patterns and rhythms of a living, spoken langage. In time, Abramovitsh was to abandon the negative view of Yiddish which he had inherited from the <u>Haskalah</u>. His mature Yiddish works not only transcend the linguistic and thematic confines of the <u>Haskalah</u> tradition, they virtually established the Yiddish novel as a serious literary genre.

Beginning in 1886, Abramovitsh returned to Hebrew literature with the publication of the short story, "The Secret Place of Thunder," and subsequently devoted himself to the translation of his Yiddish novels into Hebrew, a task which culminated in the publication of the "Jubilee Edition." Abramovitsh's translations became the occasion for significant innovations in Hebrew prose style, and for that reason, along with their pivotal influence upon the course of modern Hebrew literature, they are today considered autonomous works of art. Responding to the difficulties of translating a highly colloquial language into one that had not been spoken for nearly two thousand years, Abramovitsh abandoned the biblical pastiche that had dominated Hebrew prose and poetry for the previous hundred years and, building upon the efforts of a few early <u>Haskalah</u> writers, developed in its stead a new literary idiom based upon a synthesis of biblical, mishnaic, and medieval elements. This new Hebrew prose, celebrated by the poet Haim Nahman Bialik, among others, came to be known as the <u>nusah</u>, and exerted a powerful influence on Hebrew prose style for several generations to come.[18]

During his own lifetime Abramovitsh was known as the "grandfather" of the Hebrew (as well as the Yiddish) novel. For while his younger contemporaries recognized his roots in the earlier <u>Haskalah</u> literature, they also recognized the seminal influence of his innovations. Nor were these innovations limited to the area of Hebrew prose style. Like the writers of the <u>Haskalah</u>, Abramovitsh wrote of traditional Jewish society with sharp satire that was never entirely free of the didactic element. But, especially in his later works, he brought a new complication of tone to his treatment of Jewish life, a persistent ambivalence that Gershon Shaked has characterized as hovering between laughter and tears.[19] Abramovitsh never entirely abandoned his belief in the utilitarian function of art, but his own fiction clearly transcends the more narrow aspects of that school of thought.

Yosef Haim Brenner, as we have seen, respected Abramovitsh's artistic accomplishments, and he shared the older writer's belief in the social mission of literature. But he was also a central figure among the younger generation of writers whose works began to appear after the turn of the century and who rebelled against the "bookishness" of the <u>nusah</u> as well as the cult of social realism that Ahad Ha-Am and his Odessa school had erected around Abramovitsh's works. Brenner's generation was by no means homogeneous in its literary views and practices. Few of the most outstanding writers, for example, shared Brenner's insistence upon a literature of immediate and passionate engagement with the social ills of the day. Yet, as a group, they clearly viewed themselves as an <u>avant-garde</u> and, accordingly, the fiction writers among them experimented in matters of style, narrative technique, and choice of subject matter. In place of the measured cadences and fixed parallel structures of the <u>nusah</u>, they attempted to create a more flexible idiom by intentionally stretching or disrupting standard Hebrew syntax and opening up their prose to Yiddish, Russian, and German influences. Moreover, in place of

Abramovitsh's "everyday" Jews of the by now rapidly disintegrating traditional Jewish community in the Pale of Settlement, they turned to the uprooted Jewish intelligentsia for their protagonists. Placing a new emphasis upon the psychology and inner struggles of their protagonists, they created highly individuated and self-conscious heroes who struggle with cultural and spiritual isolation and strong intimations of approaching disaster.[20]

Like Abramovitsh, Brenner's early education was that of the heder and yeshiva. His introduction to secular subjects as well as his decision to become a writer, however, came even earlier than in Abramovitsh's case. As early as 1897, when he was only sixteen years old, Brenner wrote from Bialystok to his former yeshiva mates in Pocep of his efforts to learn Russian and German and his growing intention to abandon traditional religious studies.[21] While Brenner, like Abramovitsh, was influenced by earlier Haskalah literature, it was Russian literature that had the greatest impact upon him, particularly the criticism of V.G. Belinsky, the most important Russian literary critic of the 19th century, and the fiction of Dostoyevsky. Of the former, he wrote in 1899 to his friend at Pocep, U.N. Gnessin, "So many ideas! So much feeling! My brother I suggest you read him. He widens one's heart and improves one's taste." On Dostoyevsky's Crime and Punishment, the young Brenner had this to say to his friend and confidant: "...there are no words in my mouth to express to you my amazement at the psychological aspect of this precious and exalted book."[22] Brenner's fascination with Dostoyevsky, a volatile mixture of admiration and antipathy, continued throughout his life. His Hebrew translation of Crime and Punishment was published posthumously in 1924.

Like many writers of his generation, Brenner's youthful studies in the "forbidden" works of secular literature went hand in hand with a very early decision to become a Hebrew writer. "I want to study for another ten years or so," Brenner wrote in the same letter in which he sang the praises of Belinsky and Dostoyevsky, "and if I feel then the need and the ability -- I will write and become a writer in Israel."[23] Brenner in fact did not wait ten years; as we have seen, his first short story was published in 1900 and was followed within the next year by his collection of short stories, From the Valley of Trouble, which gained positive though qualified critical response from the established Hebrew writers and critics. With his first novella, In Winter, Brenner found his distinctive voice and established his central place in the emerging literature of the younger generation.

Brenner's travels vividly illustrate the "immigrant experience" which, according to Gershon Shaked, informs much of Hebrew literature at the turn of the century. After several years of wandering between Pocep, Bialystok, and Gomel, and two years in the Russian army, Brenner fled in 1904 to London. In 1908 he moved to Lemberg and, a year later, immigrated to Palestine. Through it all, Brenner produced numerous critical essays on literary and social topics in Hebrew and Yiddish, edited important journals that provided a platform for the younger writers, and continued to write fiction. In Palestine, Brenner was a major literary and intellectual figure, contributing to and at times editing the influential journals of the Labor Zionist factions. Brenner's uncompromising denunciations of what he considered the ideological sham of some of the official Zionist spokesmen and the intellectual pretensions of the emerging literary "establishment" of the new Jewish settlement often put him at the center of bitter controversy. Nevertheless, his passionate commitment to Jewish revival through physical labor on their own land was widely recognized; after his death in the Arab riots of 1921, the image of Brenner as a "martyr for Zion" largely overshadowed his literary accomplishment.[24] It was only in the 1960's that a new generation of literary critics in Israel rediscovered Brenner's artistry and his crucial role in the development of modern Hebrew fiction.[25]

The very length of S.Y. Agnon's career and the diversity of his literary output render classification, by generation or otherwise, an extremely difficult and perhaps not very fruitful task. In the course of more than half a century after the appearance of "Agunot," Agnon published numerous short stories, artistically recreated folktales, expressionistic pieces, novellas, and three major novels. His collected works have appeared in two editions, the first completed in 1952, the second, in eight volumes, in 1962. Since 1970, nine volumes have been published posthumously, including the novel, Shira. Still there are ample reasons to consider him a link in the chain of literary generations I have described. For although the first decades of Agnon's career coincide with the rise of the "Novel of Settlement" in Palestine, he had little in common with those writers who sought to describe, often in a crudely documentary manner, the struggles and triumphs of the emerging Jewish society in Palestine. Like the earlier writers, Agnon wrote largely about traditional Jewish society in Eastern Europe both in its vigor and decline (his birthplace, Buczacz, remained his imaginative center of focus throughout his career) and about the uprooted individuals, in Europe and Israel, of the post-traditional world. The modulations and transformations to which Agnon subjected these themes represent both a continuation and a commentary upon the earlier literature.

Agnon was also among the last great Hebrew writers of fiction of the 20th century who, in addition to modern European literary traditions, could bring to his writing a thorough knowledge of traditional Jewish literature and culture. Unlike Abramovitsh and Brenner, however, for whom the study of Russian and German represented a radical break from their traditional education and upbringing, Agnon's exposure to European literature came early and without ideological conflict. Living in Galicia, not far from the Russian border (Buczacz is now part of the Soviet Union), Agnon's family enjoyed the relative political stability, economic security, and cultural sophistication that many Jews were able to attain in the Hapsburg Empire of the latter part of the 19th century. Thus, Agnon's education combined instruction in traditional Jewish subjects, provided for the most part by private tutors, with readings in modern Hebrew and Yiddish literature, German literature, and other European literatures in German translation. Agnon's parents not only encouraged him in these readings (German literature was a particular favorite of his mother), they also encouraged his own first literary efforts in the Hebrew and Yiddish journals of Galicia.[26]

Agnon's fiction is a unique and perhaps unrepeatable synthesis of traditional Jewish and modern European elements. In his short stories and novels, the strained and self-conscious attempts at "modernism" which mark many earlier works of Hebrew fiction give way to an ironic play between traditional language and narrative modes, on the one hand, and modern narrative techniques, forms, and thematic preoccupations, on the other. In <u>A Guest for the Night</u> (1939), Agnon combines the language of piety and an anecdotal narrative style with a problematical narrative voice and global structure of motif and symbol that throw into sharp relief his (and much of modern literature's) thematic preoccupation with a lost world of spiritual and communal wholeness. In the expressionistic pieces of <u>The Book of Deeds</u> (1941), images and symbols drawn from traditional Jewish sources appear in a fragmented and phantasmagorial world where their original sense is subverted or distorted into expressions of alienation and loss.[27] The intentional archaisms of his Hebrew and the traditional qualities of his narrative style make Agnon's fiction, even in these "modernistic" works, immediately recognizable to the Hebrew reader. Yet, in spite of the central place he has occupied in Hebrew literature since the 1930's, Agnon's influence upon contemporary Israeli fiction has been limited. Even the most successful effort by a younger writer to draw upon Agnon's stylistic resources, A.B. Yehoshua's short stories of the 1960's, reveals the extent of the loss modern Hebrew literature suffered when it lost its direct link to Jewish cultural sources.

Nevertheless, modern Hebrew literature was never completely insulated from European literary and intellectual currents. From its beginning as an outgrowth of the German <u>Haskalah</u>, the very element that was modern about the literature was its writers' intent to respond to, indeed to incorporate into their own works, what they considered the best, the most progressive, or the most relevant of the cultural values and literary forms of the larger societies in which they lived. This is particularly true of the last quarter of the 19th century in Russia, the very period in which modern post-<u>Haskalah</u> Hebrew literature came of age. The influence of the Russian intellectual and literary milieu on Hebrew writers, among them Abramovitsh and Brenner, is evident in their works, in their statements about their works, as well as in the pronouncements of the Hebrew critics with whom, more often than not, they were closely associated. The questions and controversies that the Hebrew critics pursued in their literary journals not only echoed the literary controversies that preoccupied Russian intellectuals throughout the second half of the 19th century, the very terms in which the questions were posed -- truthfulness, authenticity, national spirit, social purpose -- indicate the extent to which the Russian milieu established the Hebrew critics' frame of reference and mode of argumentation.

In 1903, Ahad Ha-Am complained bitterly about what he considered this lack of originality among modern Hebrew writers:

> From the beginning of our modern literature up to the present, hardly one truly original work has appeared, a book in which our national spirit is revealed in a unique manner; almost everything is translation or imitation, and neither, in most cases, is done correctly: the translations are very far from the originals and the imitations are too close to them.[28]

Ahad Ha-Am's complaint may be somewhat exaggerated, as Gershon Shaked suggests, and it is certainly paradoxical. For even as he decried Hebrew literature's lack of originality, his own desideratum, indeed the very terminology with which he described it, reveals the degree to which his own thought was a product of "external" influences. The very concept of a "national spirit," and the notion that it is the job of literature to reveal that spirit in "a unique manner," was a central tenet of 19th-century Russian literary criticism and has its roots in the German romanticism that exerted such a powerful influence upon the Russian intelligentsia.[29] Moreover, Ahad Ha-Am's ambivalent attitude toward "external" influences -- his call for good translations but "original" imitations -- parallels the attitude of the mid-19th-century Russian "Westernizers" who, even as they eagerly absorbed and preached European ideas, looked upon Europe, as Isaiah Berlin has pointed out, with a "peculiar amalgam of love and hate."[30]

Both the Russians and the Jews looked upon their literatures as latecomers in relation to the major European literatures. As a result, they wrote about their literatures with a high degree of self-consciousness and felt acutely the need to establish their own "unique" identity even as they absorbed and refashioned European influences. Questions concerning the problems, faults, accomplishments, and potentialities of "our literature" constantly occupied the critics of each literature and the most common criterion of excellence was the "authenticity" of this or that expression of the national consciousness. In the 1840's, Belinsky could refer to Russian literature as "still an infant, albeit an infant Alcides," and could write of its need to become "more original, independent, and hence more genuine" by following Gogol's example of addressing himself "exclusively to Russian life and Russian realities."[31] Later in the century, in the "Statement of Purpose" of Hashilo'ah, the journal that was to dominate Hebrew letters for the next two decades, Ahad Ha-Am dismissed the literature of the Haskalah as a preparatory stage and called for a period of genuine cultural and literary expression. The new journal, he declared, would avoid merely "aesthetic" works that only serve to "awaken the movement of feeling for the sake of pleasure alone," and instead publish works that would contribute to a truly national literature:

> Good stories from the life of our people in the past and the present that provide authentic pictures of our situation in different times and places or that introduce a ray of light into some obscure branch of our "internal world" will thus be of great value in awakening thought and broadening national awareness among us and are therefore in line with our purpose.[32]

Ahad Ha-Am's dismissal of the merely "aesthetic" and his insistence that Hebrew literature provide "authentic pictures of our situation" also echo a major trend in 19th-century Russian literary criticism. The sine qua non of the critics who followed in Belinsky's footsteps was a literature of "truthfulness" and "authenticity." It was not enough for novelists to write of Russian life, they had to address the most pressing social issues of the day and do so with complete fidelity to the inner truths of Russian life, at least as the critics saw them. To write works that were merely pleasing, that appealed only to the reader's aesthetic sensibility, was not only a waste of time and energy, it was a betrayal of the true purpose and responsibility of the artist. Dobrolyubov and Chernyshevsky, the chief disciples of Belinsky's "social criticism," carried the conflict between the "aesthetic" and the "authentic" far beyond anything their mentor had done, but their strict utilitarian conception of art is clearly rooted in the moral stance toward literature, the belief that literature must not simply entertain but must also instruct and improve the reader, that Belinsky established and which dominated Russian literary criticism in the second half of the 19th century.[33] While Ahad Ha-Am hardly shared the revolutionary mentality of the radical Russian critics, his preference for works of literature that "awaken thought" and "broaden national awareness" is clearly rooted in the Russian intellectual milieu, though by 1896 Ahad Ha-Am's positivism was already in conflict with new developments in Russian and, as we have seen, Hebrew literature.

For the Russian critics of the 19th century, the works of Nikolai Gogol, and in particular his Dead Souls (1842), marked the beginning of the modern Russian literature of realism and authenticity and served as a model for the socially useful literature they desired. The analogous figure in modern Hebrew literature is Abramovitsh, and many of the terms and phrases that Hebrew critics used to describe his work and contribution to Hebrew literature echo what the Russian critics said about Gogol. Thus, just as Belinsky had claimed that Gogol was "the first who looked boldly and directly at Russian reality,"[34] Bialik declared that Abramovitsh was the first Hebrew writer to use his faculties of perception.[35] Brenner's admiration for the spirit of national "self-evaluation" that he found in Abramovitsh's works parallels Belinsky's concept of national "self-cognizance," which includes not only the search for the unique national spirit but a recognition of the failings and faults of contemporary society.[36] In later years, critics attempting to deal with Abramovitsh's deeply ambivalent attitude toward traditional Jewish society would write of "two Mendeles," just as the Russian critics often referred to "two Gogols."[37] The title of Gershon Shaked's book on Abramovitsh, Between Laughter and Tears (1965), is reminiscent of Pushkin's famous characterization of Gogol's art as "laughter through tears."[38]

The Hebrew critics were not simply being tendentious in ascribing, consciously or unconsciously, Gogolesque qualities to Abramovitsh's fiction. Abramovitsh was in fact deeply influenced by Gogol and it is reasonable to assume that it was from his example that Abramovitsh derived his blend of realistic attention to detail and broadly drawn caricature, his rambling narrative technique which the Russians refer to as skaz, as well as many of his standard comic devices.[39] There is an inescapable irony in the fact that the very qualities of Abramovitsh's fiction that some Hebrew and Yiddish critics have declared to be most typically Jewish are in fact the qualities most easily traced to Russian influences.

Brenner, as we have seen, was caught up in the intellectual and literary controversies of Russian literary criticism from a early age. When he urged his friend Uri Nissan Gnessin to read Belinsky, he was doing precisely what young Russian intellectuals of his time were doing. Even a half-century after his death, Belinsky remained a hero for the new generation of socially conscious youth:

> Our generation [writes a Russian scholar], born in the eighties of the last century, read the works of Belinsky with delight, as his contemporaries had done... In the happy and unhappy accidents of life the youth often gave each

other the works of Belinsky knowing that in them one could find moral support and strength.[40]

Brenner's early readings in Belinsky and the radical critics had a profound influence upon his conception of literature. While he quickly abandoned the "philanthropic" realism of his early short stories, he remained committed throughout his life to a literature of "authenticity" and social responsibility. An early letter to Gnessin, attacking his friend's attraction to "art for art's sake," vividly expresses the profoundly moral element in his demand for realism which he absorbed from the Russian milieu:

> In regard to your theory in your letter concerning "literature for literature's sake" and the purpose of man, etc., I do not agree at all. My world view is entirely different. In short: we must sacrifice our souls in order to reduce evil in the world, the evil of hunger, slavery, idleness, hypocrisy, and so forth. It is imperative to understand everything, to understand and to avoid mysticism and fantasy; it is imperative to strengthen realism and holiness in the world; it is imperative to improve the life of the Jewish nation so that it can be normal. The terrible agonies of my soul are the result of my doubts about everything. Is it still possible to mend our ways?[41]

Brenner's objection to Ahad Ha-Am's positivism and "objective" social realism, then, was not based upon an opposing concept of the function of literature. Ahad Ha-Am and Brenner agreed on the essentially moral purpose of literature. Brenner, however, insisted that the purpose could be served only by a literature that authentically revealed the intensely personal and subjective inner world of the "uprooted" individuals of the new generation as they struggled with ideologies and emotions toward an affirmation, however circumscribed, of life. Brenner's preface to his novel, <u>From Here and There</u>, sounds like a direct repudiation of the kind of realism Ahad Ha-Am called for in the first issue of <u>Hashilo'ah</u>:

> This realism... is not that wide-ranging, all encompassing, totalistic naturalism, nor that supreme realism that raises itself to an overview of the spectacle of life, realism that does not describe what is but what should or could be, etc., etc., but rather -- alas! -- simple realism, wing-clipped, crawling realism, photographic realism.[42]

Brenner's intellectual and artistic debt to Dostoyevsky has long been recognized and has, indeed, become the subject of numerous studies and critical essays.[43] Dostoyevsky's influence on Brenner, moreover, did not escape the attention of his contemporaries. Responding to an early work, Bialik felt it necessary to insist, rather vaguely, upon the influence of "our own writers" on the young artist, even as he pointed out Brenner's obvious affinities to Dostoyevsky.[44] But while Dostoyevsky's influence upon Brenner was considerable, it was by no means unique. The ideological struggles of Brenner's heroes, even those who have made the move to Palestine, are rooted in the ideological and spiritual ferment of pre-revolutionary Russia. Feuermann, the hero of <u>In Winter</u>, struggles with the pronouncements of Pisarev, Dostoyevsky, Tolstoy, Checkov, and Gorky, and has a dream in which he confronts Nietzsche in Germany. Yehezkel Hefetz, the hero of Breakdown and Bereavement, has that confrontation through an imagined debate with his arch-enemy, Himilin, the final avatar of the Nietzschean "villain" that both attracts and repells most of Brenner's protagonists.[45]

It is far more difficult to specify direct influences upon Agnon's fiction than it is in the case of Abramovitsh and Brenner. This is not the result, however, of a lack of such influences. Born into the relative freedom and tranquility of Hapsburg Galicia, Agnon did not share the specifically Russian concerns of the two older writers, but his contact with European literature was considerably more extensive and prolonged. In addition to his early readings in Buczacz, Agnon read extensively in German, Scandinavian, and Russian literature (the last two in German translation) during his first stay in Jaffa. In Germany, where he lived from 1912 to 1924, he received from his friend and patron, Salmon Schocken, books by, among others, Balzac, Dostoyevsky, Zola, Flaubert, Romain Rolland, and August Strindberg. In his letters to Schocken, Agnon expressed particular admiration for Flaubert's dedication to his craft. "Every writer," he wrote, "should read about him before he writes and after he writes..."[46] Of Strindberg's autobiographical writings, he wrote, "From the poetic side they did not please me. But from the human side they taught me a lesson. Most of the torments that he had in his relations with people (except for women) I have felt and feel in my own flesh."[47] In response to questions concerning the manner and extent to which his readings in European literature influenced his own works, Agnon has been typically reticent, at times rather cagey. There are, however, inescapable parallels between some of Agnon's works published during and after the 1930's, particularly the short works collected in The Book of Deeds, and the writings of Kafka, although the precise nature of those parallels has been the subject of heated debate and, as Arnold Band points out, Agnon wrote what could be called "Kafkaesque" fiction as early as 1907.[48] Agnon's own response to the question of Kafka's influence is couched in his characteristic ironic mode. While he claimed to have read "barely two books" by Kafka, and did not like what he read, he went on to say that his wife admired the German author and kept a set of his complete works in her library.[49]

* * *

"Of the critical controversies that nourished the literature of the [nineteenth] century," writes Rufus W. Mathewson, Jr. in his classic study of the "positive" hero in Russian literature, "none was more intense than the discussion about the kind of significance that should be invested in the figure of the literary hero."[50] The Russian social critics, for whom the boundary between life and literature was in any event rather ill-defined, generally analyzed literary heroes as if they were dealing with real people, and judged them, either for praise or blame, by the same standards and with the same degree of passion that one generally reserves for friends or enemies. Moreover, they tried to find in these characters the specific imprint of the Russian political and social environment, and thus the characters they found most interesting, if not necessarily the most attractive, were the ones who most accurately and vividly embodied aspects of the

Russian "national character." In his essay on Goncharov's <u>Oblomov</u> (1859), Dobrolyubov wrote not so much of Oblomov, the lethargic and ineffectual hero of the novel, but of what he called "Oblomovitis," a set of character traits that he also found in Pushkin's Eugene Onegin, Lermontov's Pechorin, and Turgenev's Rudin, and which, more importantly for Dobrolyubov, was "a product of Russian life, a sign of the times."[51] The controversy surrounding Turgenev's "nihilist" hero of <u>Fathers and Sons</u> (1862) proceeded along similar lines. While most of the young radicals rejected Bazarov as an unflattering caricature, Pisarev declared that "if Bazarovism is a malady, it is the malady of our time."[52] For Chernyschevsky, the "base behavior" of the hero of Turgenev's short story "Asya" is "nothing other than a symptom of the epidemic disease rooted in our society."[53]

The controversy over the literary hero centered around two "types," one which the radical critics found in great abundance in Russian literature up to their day, and another which they hoped to see emerge as a result of the developing social consciousness which they saw (or hoped to create) in Russian society. Thus, on the one hand, there were what came to be called the "superfluous" men, the heroes struck with "Oblomovitis," who, as a result of the political and social backwardness of Russian society, were reduced to banal and trivial concerns or, insofar as they attempted and invariably failed in some positive action, to hopelessness, physical lethargy, and spiritual paralysis. Held up against the "superfluous man" was the positive hero, the "new man" whose appearance in literature and life was eagerly awaited by the radical critics. This hero, thanks to his new "civic consciousness," would rise above the mediocrity of his education and surroundings and take direct action against the ills of Russian society.

The question of the literary hero, of course, was only one aspect of the larger debate that preoccupied Russian social and literary criticism in the second half of the 19th century. The real issue was the significance and function of literature itself, and the notion of a positive hero was, as Mathewson points out, a "weapon of argument" in this debate.[54] Thus, for radical critics like Dobrolyubov and Chernyshevsky, while the "superfluous" man had effectively revealed the deleterious effects of the "banality" of Russian society, a positive hero who could show the way to social and political action was now required if literature were to continue to fulfill its utilitarian function. Writers like Turgenev and, before his "conversion" in 1880, Tolstoy, had little faith in the radical critics' simplistic blueprint for a positive hero. Though they attempted on occasion to create positive heroes of their own, they also insisted upon art's independence from the prescriptions of political movements or ideologies, the autonomy of the personal artistic vision, and the artist's obligation to present "the whole truth," not partial, one-sided, or tendentious versions of it.

None of this was lost on the Hebrew writers and critics who, as we have seen, were thoroughly caught up in the intellectual turmoil of the Russian milieu. Thus, their concerns over the possibility of creating an "authentic" Jewish literature, one in which the "national spirit is revealed in a unique manner," often centered upon the question of the Jewish hero. If such a literature could be created, they asked, how would it differ from the literatures of other nations? And, in particular, how would the Jewish hero or heroine differ from the heroes and heroines of other literatures?[55] Thus, following the example of the Russian critics, the Hebrew critics analyzed the heroes that appeared in the literature as embodiments of national types or "symptoms" of social, political, or cultural developments in Jewish society. The controversy between those who, like Bialok, saw in Abramovitsh the first Hebrew realist, and dissenters from this view, like Shelomo Tsemah, revolved around the "truthfulness" of Abramovitsh's broadly drawn caricatures and whether they accurately represented the "Jewish human being."[56] Similarly the controversy over Brenner's heroes was fought out between those who saw in them simply "miserable adolescents and loafers" and those who considered them "genuine representatives of the new generation."[57] The heated controversies that animated Hebrew literary criticism around the turn of the century, and which continued to dominate Israeli literary criticism as well into the 1950's, owe both their preoccupations and their particular flavor to the Russian milieu. Like the Russian critics of the second half of the 19th century, the Hebrew critics blurred the boundary between literature and life, analyzed literary heroes as embodiments of national types, and responded to them in a highly personal and often passionate manner, as if they were real people.

The heroes that the critics responded to in this fashion and in whom they sought to discover the unique features of the Jewish hero were themselves, to a large degree, constructed according to Russian models. Abramovitsh's rejection of the heroic stereotypes of Romantic fiction on the grounds that Jewish society in the Pale of Settlement provided no models for such heroes is reminiscent of Belinsky's explanation of the lack of Romantic heroes in Russian literature in the 1840's. Such heroes, Belinsky argued, had no place in Russian literature because they could not be found in Russian life during what he considered the period of "stagnation" in which he lived.[58] Similarly, Reb Shelomo, the autobiographical hero of Abramovitsh's In Those Days, "complains" of the absence of "dukes, governors, generals, and warriors" in Jewish society, a society in which, according to him, "the behavior of all its members... is determined by a single formula."[59] Abramovitsh's substitution of grotesquely caricatured "national types" for the Romantic hero as well as his propensity to view the formulaic behavior of these types in biological terms and metaphors accord well with Belinsky's pronouncements and with the practice of Gogol, whose characters Belinsky considered unique expressions of the Russian national consciousness.

Nor is the talush or "uprooted man," who figures so prominently in the novels of Brenner and others of his generation, a uniquely Jewish phenomenon. He is, to a large degree, the Jewish avatar of the Russian "superfluous man" who, according to Mathewson, was to become "one of the most durable clichés in Russian literary criticism."[60] The definitive traits of the superfluous man as he appears in various forms and stages of development from Turgenev's "Diary of a Superfluous Man" (and some would argue, along with Dobrolyubov, from Eugene Onegin[61]) to Dostoyevsky's Notes From Underground and beyond, -- his failure to find purpose in life or a basis for hope, his predilection for defeat, his alienation from other human beings, his inability to pursue purposeful activity

-- are present in the Hebrew _talush_. When H.Y. Katzenelson described the protagonist of Brenner's first novella, _In Winter_, as a "superfluous, broken, uprooted man," in the Russian Jewish press, he was using a set of terms quite familiar to his readers and which, in Hebrew translation, would become as durable a cliché as it already was in Russian literary criticism.[62] In his novel _Only Yesterday_, Agnon subjects this cliché to a radical reinterpretation. Dividing the traits of the "uprooted" between a spiritually lethargic human protagonist and a hyper-conscious canine, Agnon generates a sophisticated parody which "exposes" the cliché while investing the tradition with new meanings.

The novels of Abramovitsh, Brenner, and Agnon, then, are especially pertinent to a study that focuses upon the literary hero. As a result of the special circumstances in which the novelists pursued their work as well as the "external" influences they absorbed, all three shared a preoccupation with the question of the hero. Thus, an analysis of the protagonists in some of their most characteristic novels should prove an effective means of access to their larger formal and thematic concerns. As we shall see, the novelists' approach to the question of the protagonist and his function differed significantly, and, in some cases, dramatically. Thus, a study of these novels provides us, as well, with a unique opportunity to view the radical shifts that can take place in the representation of the literary hero within a relatively short span of time. Finally, a study of this sort provides an opportunity to raise some fundamental questions concerning the general issue of character in narrative fiction. Even if we grant that Abramovitsh, Brenner, and Agnon shared to varying degrees the critics' predilection for "real" and "representative" heroes, is the approach that treats literary heroes as though they were real people necessarily the best or most illuminating mode of analysis? What can we learn if we insist upon maintaining -- as the Russian and Hebrew critics we have discussed did not -- a strict demarcation between life and literature, and rather than attempting to reveal the protagonist's relation to life, we attempt to reveal his relation to literature, that is, to the specifically literary qualities of the narrative structure in which he appears? It is to an examination of this question as it has surfaced in literary theory over the last two decades that the next chapter is devoted.

CHAPTER TWO
Is There A Person In The Text?

An interest in fiction, it seems safe to say, presupposes an interest in people. Indeed, we often read novels for the sake of the "memorable characters" we hope to find in them. Long after the particulars of plot and theme may be forgotten, such characters are likely to remain vividly imprinted in our memory. Whatever we may think of the characters in a novel, we seldom remain indifferent to them. We love them or we hate them, we follow their stories with keen interest or we are bored by them, we condemn their behavior, or we attempt to understand and forgive. And when we attempt to understand, we invariably find ourselves drawing upon the same techniques, concepts, and terms that we use when we attempt to understand friends, acquaintances, or historical figures.

Now when fictional characters are treated in this manner, it is a relatively simple operation to take them "off the page." Fictional characters become, or seem to become, autonomous beings, independent of the text that bore them. We may speculate about a character's past, even if that past is not described or alluded to in the narrative in which he appears. Or we may place the character in situations not mentioned in the text and consider how he might respond, given what we already "know" about him. A character's feelings, thoughts, attitudes, and motives, whether explicitly described in the narrative or not, all seem fair game for our speculation. While we may have a certain intuitive sense as to where such speculation goes beyond the boundaries of "legitimate" interpretation, we would be hard pressed indeed to define the exact location of those boundaries.

This way of dealing with fictional characters, however natural it may appear, is clearly based upon certain expectations we bring to our reading. Fiction, according to the conventions of realism that have dominated its writing at least since the latter part of the eighteenth century, provides us with an image of life, or at least a recognizable analogy to it.[1] How natural, then, to pursue that analogy in relation to the characters that appear in fiction. Indeed, the conventions of realism are so firmly entrenched, the expectations they promote so thoroughly internalized, that even when a character deviates from human experience as we understand it, our first response is to "naturalize" the apparent deviation. Depth psychology, sociology, history, folk wisdom, or even the "enigmatic" nature of Man may all be invoked in this process. But, by whatever means, we insist that the character be made to conform to our notions about reality and the way people deal with it.

Nor is there any lack of sophisticated literary analysts who confirm the legitimacy of what, after all, appears to be common practice. Marvin Mudrick, for example, has argued that since fictional characters "acquire, in the course of an action, a kind of independence from the events in which they live... they can be usefully discussed at some distance from their context."[2] Indeed, Mudrick goes on to compare fictional characters with historical figures, both of which, according to him, "share a bounty of individual vitality that lifts them dolphin-like out of the element they live in" (218). More recently, Seymour Chatman has suggested that "some orthographic device, like quotation marks," is sufficient to distinguish between the imputed traits of fictional characters and the real traits of real people.[3]

Mudrick and Chatman argue in favor of the "willing suspension of disbelief" that realist conventions demand. Fictional characters are not real people, they seem to say, but both the intentions of novelists and the process of reading itself seem to confirm that this fact, once noted, can be safely ignored. Thus, following the logic of his argument, Chatman turns to those who make a science of studying real people for help in developing his own approach to the analysis of fictional characters. Taking his definition of character from the <u>Dictionary of Philosophy</u>, he derives his analytical procedures from an impressive selection of essays dealing with psychological theories of personality. Were Chatman to take his argument one step further, he would have to conclude that philosophers and psychologists, not literary critics, are best qualified to deal with fictional characters. And, in fact, many literary critics seem to have drawn this conclusion. Their analyses of fictional characters are often based upon a more or less sophisticated knowledge of psychological theories, usually Freudian, or else they cede the field entirely to "psychoanalytical literary critics."[4]

But what if we choose, for the sake of argument, not to suspend our disbelief in the "reality" of fictional characters? Surely the fact that fictional characters are not real people is, at least potentially, a significant one. What conclusions might result from such a consideration? And how might those conclusions affect our analytical procedures?

There are a number of obstacles to such a consideration. For one thing, there have been, until relatively recently, few systematic theoretical analyses of the specific nature of fictional characters, of the ways in which they differ from real people, and the implications such differences may have for literary analysis.[5] This may be due, in part at least, to the traditional lack of interest among Anglo-American literary critics in "theoretical" matters. But even if we can now easily recognize many of the purely literary conventions involved in the production and consumption of realistic fiction, fictional characters still pose a special problem. They still seem the least "literary" element of narrative fiction, the one most firmly anchored in reality. We have, for example, an ample arsenal of concepts and terms with which to deal with plot; plots, after all, do not exist, strictly speaking, other than in fiction. "People," on the other hand, exist both in life and in literature, or at least they seem to exist in the latter as well as the former. Thus, an attempt to distinguish between fictional characters and real people is bound to be more complex than distinguishing, for example, between story and discourse.

One notable attempt to develop a vocabulary to deal with the specific nature of fictional characters was made by E.M. Forster in his <u>Aspects of the Novel</u>. Forster's famous distinction between "flat" and "round" characters, however, has suffered an unfortunate fate, for the terms passed with such ease into the critical vocabulary -- a fact that is perhaps indicative of the felt need for an expanded terminology -- that their use often became quite mechanical, serving as an end to discussion rather than a starting point. And for this reason, the terms have been dismissed as crude, simplistic, or at best excessively abstract. But they deserve a better fate. For Forster did not introduce his terms simply to identify two different "types" of characters; for him, they describe two "devices" through which novelists attempt to resolve the fundamental tension involved in the creation of fictional characters, the tension between the demands of mimesis and the requirements of art. And it is in this context that the terms must be understood.

Forster takes it for granted that there is "bound to be a difference" between fictional characters and real people.[6] This difference, according to Forster, stems from the fact that we can simply know more about a fictional character than we can ever know about even our most intimate acquaintances. Specifically, the inner life of a fictional character -- his unexpressed thoughts, emotions, motives -- can be revealed by the novelist, whereas this sphere of human activity remains largely hidden in our everyday intercourse with other people. Indeed, if the novelist so wishes, we can know everything about a fictional character that is worth knowing, everything that is necessary to achieve a "perfect knowledge" of him. Thus, Forster concludes, "the reality we get in a novel is of a kind we can never get in daily life" (70).

The author of a novel can, of course, choose to tell us much less about his characters than would be required for this perfect knowledge. This decision, however, is not an arbitrary one, for the author must, according to Forster, present his characters in conformity to the requirements of his work as a whole. The creation and presentation of fictional characters, then, involve a process of "adaptation" and "acclimatization." Fictional characters, however their existence may parallel everyday life, must also adapt -- or be adapted -- to the "other requirements of their creator."

> The characters arrive when evoked, but full of the spirit of mutiny. For they have these numerous parallels with people like ourselves, they try to live their own lives and are consequently often engaged in treason against the main scheme of the book. They "run away," they "get out of hand"; they are creations inside a creation, and often inharmonious towards it; if they are given complete freedom, they kick the book to pieces, and if they are kept too sternly in check, they revenge themselves by dying, and destroy it by intestinal decay. (74)

The tension that Forster describes here is similar to the tension that the Russian Formalists had earlier described as that between "realistic motivation" and "artistic motivation."[7] The Russian Formalists, however, were chiefly interested in how these often conflicting motivations influenced plot structure. For Forster, what is at issue here is the tension between a "realistic" presentation of character as demanded by mimetic conventions (individuality, freedom, etc.) and the need of the author to present his characters according to the "main scheme of the book," that is, according to the requirements of the overall narrative structure.

What Forster is emphasizing, finally, is the fact that fictional characters, unlike real people, are constructs, "creations within a creation." Thus, the relative "flatness" or "roundness" of a particular character is determined, ultimately, by the requirements of the narrative in which he appears.

> ...by using it (the round character) sometimes alone, more often in combination with the other kind, the novelist achieves his task of acclimatization, and harmonizes the human race with the other aspects of his work. (85)

Rather than simply labeling characters as "flat" or "round," we must ask why a particular character is presented as he is. What purpose or function does the particular mode of characterization serve in terms of the "main scheme of the book?" "There may be more to flatness," Forster notes, "than the severe critics admit" (79).

It may seem rather impertinent to link E.M. Forster with a group of literary theorists who dismiss the very notion of realism as at best an illusion, at worst a critical fallacy of the highest order. Indeed, the "narratologists" usually associated with the various branches of Structuralism are often accused of brutally dehumanizing literature and, in the case of fictional characters, tendentiously excluding them from the proper realm of literary analysis. Yet, emerging from a very different critical tradition, and proceeding from assumptions that would no doubt have been anathema to the humanist Forster, the Structuralists have provided us with a systematic and fruitful discussion of the questions raised by Forster concerning fictional characters.

Indeed, one might argue that the Structuralists' devaluation of notions about personal identity in life as well as literature, their dismissal of individuality as an "historical trope" rapidly passing from the scene, have had, whatever the validity of such claims, a liberating effect in regard to literary analysis. For this point of view has prompted them to deal with fictional characters as constructs, rather than simply more or less accurate representations of human beings as we know them, or believe we know them. Moreover, their insistence upon viewing narratives as structures -- arrangements of elements embodying the ideas of wholeness, transformation, and self-regulation[8] -- requires them to analyze fictional characters in relation to, in Forster's terms, "the main scheme of the book." Thus, Roland Barthes defines the basic approach of the Structuralists toward fictional characters:

> Anxious not to define character in terms of psychological essence, structural analysis has so far attempted, through various hypotheses, to define character as a "participant" rather than as a "being."[9]

As "participants," or elements of a larger narrative structure, fictional characters, the Structuralists claim, should be analyzed and defined according to the function they perform in that structure. Thus, rather than pursuing the parallels between fictional characters and real people, indeed denying the very significance of such parallels, the Structuralists examine the interrelationships between characters and the other elements of the narrative structure in which they participate.

Before examining some of the results of this approach, we should note that the Structuralists have, by and large, not dealt directly or specifically with the problem of fictional characters. Their primary interest has been the analysis of the most distinctive and, they would claim, the definitive element of narrative discourse, namely, the organization of actions and events along the narrative syntagm. Their insights into fictional characters, in fact, may be seen as the by-product of their efforts in this area. For this reason, their work has been especially disconcerting to readers and critics for whom the unfolding of character, rather than plot, remains the primary interest of fiction. Indeed, it may be claimed that, at least in practice, the Structuralists set up a false hierarchy in which characters are reduced to mere functions or by-products of plot. But if the Structuralists set up such a hierarchy, they also provide us with the means to reverse or dismantle it.[10] In any event, our interest here is not in the canonical form of this or that Structuralist analysis, but in an approach to narrative structure which, in spite of the much heralded arrival of Post-structuralism, is still in the process of formation, indeed still in its infancy.

Since the work of the Russian Formalists provided much of the inspiration for later structural analyses of narrative and, to a large degree, established the basic direction of those analyses, it will be useful to examine some of their methodological assumptions insofar as they relate to the question of fictional character before turning to the Structuralists themselves. Moreover, unhampered by the neologistic penchants and rhetorical affectations displayed by some of the later Structuralists, the Russians provide us with a relatively clear exposition of their, and the later Structuralists', working hypotheses.

In his essay, "Thematics," Boris Tomashevsky presents a useful summary of the Russian Formalists' approach to narrative fiction. The analysis of narrative must begin, according to Tomashevsky, by identifying the most fundamental and therefore irreducible narrative unit. In Formalist terminology, this unit, "the smallest particle of thematic material," is called a "motif," and two basic categories of motifs can be identified.[11] Motifs that cannot be omitted from the story without destroying its coherence are called "bound motifs." Such motifs are strictly narrative in character, that is, they denote actions, events, or incidents. All other motifs, including those that deal exclusively with characterization, are called "free motifs," and they can be omitted since the coherence of the story is not dependent upon them.

Insofar as characters, as such, are recognized in a narrative, it is by means of a "system" of free motifs scattered among the bound motifs along the narrative syntagm. A free motif may be no more than a name, or it may be a passage of external description of a character, or the attribution of more or less complex psychological characteristics. But since these free motifs are not essential to the coherence of the story, their only requirement is that they "be appropriate to the story." Otherwise, for the purposes of Formalist analysis at least, they can be ignored. "The story, as a system of motifs, can dispense entirely with [the protagonist] and his characteristics" (90).

While characters are not necessary to the story they do, however, perform some useful functions. "The character," Tomashevsky writes, "is the guiding thread that makes it possible to untangle a conglomeration of motifs and permits them to be classified and arranged" (88). Thus, the character is no more than a "device for grouping and stringing together motifs" (87). The relationship between various bound motifs can, for example, be clarified by reference to the character or characters who perform the actions they denote. One may argue that on this basis characters, even as devices, are necessary for the coherence of the story. For Tomashevsky, however, they may be useful, but are by no means essential.

The distinction between "bound" and "free" motifs clearly rests upon the assumption that actions and events, not characters, are the real stuff of narrative. While such a hierarchical distinction may have a certain methodological value, the implications of this approach for the study of fictional characters do not seem very promising. Either a character is created by an independent system of free motifs largely irrelevant to the structure of the story, or else the character is simply the incidental though not unuseful by-product of the relations between bound motifs. In either case, serious discussion of the interrelations between story and character, the ways in which character attributes, for example, may determine plot developments or be affected by them, seems to be precluded.

Nevertheless, by their insistence upon viewing characters as "devices," that is, in terms of the function they serve (or do not serve) in the narrative structure, the Russian Formalists established the functional analysis of fictional characters as the central aim of subsequent Structuralist analysis of characters. Even the emotional attitude we may have toward the protagonist of a novel, Tomashevsky reminds us, "is set by his function in the work." "An author may arouse sympathy for a protagonist whose character in real life would provoke revulsion and disgust. The emotional attitude toward the protagonist is a fact of the artistic construction of the tale..." (90).

A major contribution toward such a functional analysis of fictional characters was made by Vladimir Propp in his study of the Russian folktale. Indeed, his work is often viewed as the link between the Russian Formalists and the later Structuralists, the latters' work representing an attempt to apply and refine Propp's basic insights and categories.[12] In his *Morphology of the Russian Folktale*, Propp applies the Russian Formalists' notion of the motif -- he uses the term "function" -- to a limited corpus of Russian folktales. A function, according to Propp, is an "act of a character defined from the point of view of its significance for the course of the action of the tale as a whole."[13] Through a process of abstraction Propp is able to reduce the functions found in the tales he considers to a finite and relatively small number. Thus, in the one hundred folktales he analyzes, he identifies thirty-one distinct functions. Moreover, he discovered that the appearance of these functions in the individual tales follows certain definite patterns. Thus, while no single tale includes all thirty-one functions, those that did appear always did so in the same order. From the point of view of functions, then, Propp can conclude that "all fairy tales are of one type in regard to their structure" (23).

Propp also discovered that the thirty-one functions could be organized into seven "spheres of action" distributed among the personages appearing in the various tales. As a result, the personages in the tales could be identified and defined in terms of the sphere of action (the specific configuration of functions) associated with them. From the large variety of individual characters, then, Propp derives the following "functional" roles: 1) villain; 2) donor (provider); 3) helper; 4) princess (a sought-after person) and her father, 5) dispatcher; 6) hero (seeker or victim); and 7) false hero (79-83).

From the point of view of a structural analysis of fictional characters, Propp's functional analysis is highly significant. For one thing, he provides us with a set of categories and terms derived from the functions the characters fulfill in the narrative structure, rather than from parallels in real life. Moreover, these categories make possible a typological analysis through which a large number of characters can be compared and contrasted in terms of a limited number of roles. Thus, as Propp points out, in any given tale one character may play several different roles and, conversely, several characters may fulfill the same role.

Unlike Tomashevsky, then, Propp does not exclude characters from the basic structure of narrative; on the contrary, only when characters are identified in terms of their role can the structure of a tale or group of tales emerge. Yet, like Tomashevsky, characters are analyzed exclusively in terms of their actions and, moreover, only actions that are significant "for the course of the action of the tale as a whole." Thus, the specific attributes of characters are irrelevant or, at least, nonessential in regard to the overall structure of the narrative. The role of villain, for example, may be played equally well by a dragon, a witch, a giant, or any evil person or creature. Propp is willing to admit that the specific attributes of a character -- age, sex, external appearance, etc. -- "provide the tale with its brilliancy, charm, and beauty" (87). But again, for the purposes of his analysis of narrative, these attributes are merely contingent and of no structural significance.

Propp, as we have seen, worked inductively from a limited corpus of Russian folktales, and while the results of his analysis clearly have applications beyond that corpus, he makes no claim for the universality of his categories. A.J. Greimas, on the other hand, has attempted to recast Propp's categories in terms of a universally applicable model of narrative based upon what he considers the "elementary structure of signification," the binary opposition.[14] As in the case of all human thought and its products (most notably, language), the binary opposition, according to Greimas, underlies and generates the superficial surface structure of all narratives. Details may differ, the content of actions and the attributes of characters may vary, but the grammar of narrative discourse -- the "enunciation spectacle" -- remains constant, just as the grammar of a language remains constant from sentence to sentence.

At the level of deep structure, then, all narratives are based upon a fundamental oppositional structure, and the essence of narrative lies in the manner in which this opposition is modified or resolved. At the surface level of narrative, these opposed elements are manifested in "actants" (roughly analogous to Propp's "spheres of action"), and the modification or resolution of the opposition will, on this level, involve the transfer of some entity -- an object, person, quality -- from one actantial plane to another.[15]

Basing his analysis, in part, on Propp's work, Greimas provides an inventory of actants which, abstracted and regularized, can be applied, according to Greimas, to all narratives, not just the relatively simple folktale. Moreover, in order to emphasize the structural (i.e., oppositional) relationship between the actants, he organizes them into three sets of binary oppositions. Thus, in place of Propp's seven spheres of action, we get three "actantial categories":

1. Subject vs. Object
2. Sender vs. Receiver
3. Helper vs. Opponent (176-180)

Whatever the advantages of this configuration, Greimas' actantial analysis represents a refinement of, not a departure from, the results of Propp's inductive analysis. As in the case of Propp, characters are analyzed and defined in terms of their function in the overall narrative structure, according, in other words, to the actant they represent or embody. And, as in Propp's analysis, it follows that several characters (Greimas prefers to call them actors), whatever the apparent differences between them, may be nothing more than varying articulations of the same actant, and thus structurally identical. Or, on the other hand, one character may embody several otherwise independent actants. Whatever the case, a character is identified not according to his specific traits or attributes, but according to the role he plays in the fundamental oppositional structure of the narrative in which he appears.

Whatever the merits or deficiencies of the systems proposed by Propp and Greimas, if we grant that there is a need for a set of terms and categories that will enable us to analyze fictional characters in terms of their narrative function, their work is surely a significant step in this direction. For rather than viewing fictional characters as simply opportunities for mimetic portraiture, they view them as constructs or devices which serve specific narrative functions. To put it in the most positive terms, an actantial analysis of fictional characters can liberate us from the notion that all characters in all fiction can and indeed must be analyzed in terms of their greater or lesser fidelity to our knowledge of human behavior. Such an anlysis might show that even characters who conform to our extra-literary experience may be most profitably analyzed not in terms of that experience, but in terms of their function in the work in which they appear. As Terence Hawkes points out, it is clearly useful to see that, in terms of their function in the structure of *King Lear*, Cordelia and the Fool are embodiments of a single actantial plane.[16]

But the example of Cordelia and the Fool also points to the greatest weakness of the actantial analysis of fictional characters. For once one has identified the functional similarity between diverse characters, once, that is, they have been placed in the proper actantial category, the differences between the characters may still be significant. Yet these differences have no place in the actantial analysis since they are viewed as merely contingent surface structures. It is, for example, surely of some significance that Lear's passage to the actantial plane to which Cordelia and the Fool belong is accompanied by his decline into madness. An adequate structural analysis of *King Lear*, one would presume, would be able to account for the role played by madness. But, as Jonathan Culler argues, "the roles proposed [by Propp, Greimas, and others] are so reductive and so directly dependent upon plot that they leave us with an immense residue whose organization structural analysis should attempt to explain rather than ignore."[17]

One might argue that the usefulness of structural analysis in which characters are identified and defined solely according to their function in the plot is limited to works in which plot, rather than character, is given primacy, as in the folktales analyzed by Propp. Tzvetan Todorov, for example, chose to deal with the Decameron in his analysis of the "grammar" of narrative precisely because, as he explains, the plots of the individual tales are "relatively simple" yet "play a dominant role" and involve no more than three or four characters.[18] Such tales, Todorov eventually concludes, may contain specific "attributional propositions" which may be relevant to the structure of the plot (60), but propositions that indicate psychological motivation (of which there are few in the Decameron) are always considered "optional." For while such propositions may provide the "salt of the story," they are "not necessary to our perception of the novella's plot as a completed whole."[19]

Todorov, to be sure, recognizes the existence of other types of narrative in which psychological motivation provides more than the "salt of the story," in which psychological motivation may in fact be as important or more important than the purely "syntactic" elements. At the beginning of his essay, "Narrative-Men," for example, he quotes Henry James' famous statements on the relationship between character and incident:

> What [James asks] is character but the determination of incident? What is incident but the illustration of character? What is either a picture or a novel that is not of character? What else do we seek in it and find in it?[20]

What bothers Todorov about James' statement is not that it is incorrect, at least in regard to the kind of fiction that James wrote, but that James seems to be talking about all narrative, when he is really only describing one "tendency," namely, psychological narrative. Such narratives, Todorov is willing to admit, "regard each action as a means of access to the personality in question, as an expression if not a symptom. Action is not considered in itself, but is transitive with regard to its subject" (67). But there is, Todorov insists, another kind of narrative -- of which the Decameron, as well as the Odyssey, the Arabian Nights, and the Saragossa Manuscript are examples -- in which this is not the case. In such narratives:

> ...the actions are not there to illustrate character but... on the contrary, the characters are subservient to the action... moreover the word "character" signifies something altogether different from psychological coherence or the description of idiosyncrasy. (66)

It is the latter type of narrative, as we have seen, that Todorov prefers to deal with for the sake of methodological rigor.

But if it is a question of two tendencies, indeed two types of narrative, then it will be of utmost importance to identify the characteristics that set them apart. The distinctive feature of "a-psychological narrative," according to Todorov, is not the absence of explicit character analysis, but rather the nature of the relationship between attributive propositions and propositions that denote action. That relationship, Todorov observes, is always one of immediate causality: every notation of an explicit attribute is always followed immediately by a specific action. As a result, the attributive proposition is deprived "of any autonomy, of an intransitive meaning." It becomes, in effect, merely the iterative aspect of the non-iterative proposition of action (68).

The ultimate test as to whether a particular narrative is a-psychological or psychological, however, involves the question of psychological coherence. "Actions provoke one another, and as a by-product a psychological cause and effect coupling appears, but on a different level" (69). Only if these psychological "by-products" can be integrated into a psychologically coherent whole, if they can be shown to "form a system," only then we are dealing with psychological narrative. Todorov cites the tale of Ali Baba from the <u>Arabian Nights</u> as an example of narrative in which the psychological by-products do not cohere. Kassim's wife's sudden shift from grief over her husband's grisly death (Ali Baba has brought her pieces of her husband's corpse!) to joy over Ali Baba's offer of marriage makes little sense, at least in the realm of "commonsense" psychology. One could, of course, speculate as to the existence of hidden motives for her behavior, or attempt to explain it in terms of abnormal psychology. But Todorov's point is that this kind of speculation would represent a deviation from the folkloristic norms of the <u>Arabian Nights</u>; it would be forcing psychological motivation into what is, in fact, an a-psychological narrative in which "action is important in itself and not as an indication of this or that character trait" (67).

Todorov's use of the term "tendency" in relation to a-psychological and psychological narratives is significant, for it suggests that many narratives will exhibit both tendencies in varying proportions. In such mixed narratives, the decision whether to focus the analysis upon the syntactic aspect, i.e., the organization of the actions, or upon the psychology of the characters may well depend upon the predilections of the analyst. One can, for example, isolate and analyze the narrative syntax of a nineteenth-century psychological narrative; one can also analyze the personality of Odysseus. In either case, however, the analysis would only be a partial one, and, moreover effectively break the "unbreakable link" between action and character about which Todorov and James are apparently in agreement. Todorov avoids this danger by choosing "simple" a-psychological narratives as the object of his analysis, but, clearly, defining the nature of that link represents a major challenge to Structuralist analysis if it is to deal successfully with the major narrative forms of the last two centuries.

Roland Barthes apparently takes up this challenge in <u>S/Z</u> in which he presents a detailed and systematic analysis of Balzac's "Sarrasine," which he describes as a "classically" realistic tale. Now while <u>S/Z</u> has become a central text of Structuralist analysis, it is important to note that, by Barthes' own definition, it is not an example of "pure" structural analysis, but rather what Barthes prefers to call "textual analysis." The object of structural analysis, Barthes observes, is to reveal the common structure underlying all narrative by observing the "systematic correlation of terms denoting action."[21] Textual analysis, on the other hand, "endeavors to 'see' each text in its difference."[22] The text is viewed as a "production of significance," and rather than showing how the text is made, the goal of textual analysis is to show "how it is unmade, how it explodes, disseminates -- by what coded paths it goes off" (127).

In order to do this, Barthes must transgress the "rule of immanence" under which, according to him, purely structural analysis must operate and direct his attention instead to the "narrative situation," the knowledge and experience which the reader brings to the act of reading.[23] Now the "narrative situation" is, according to Barthes, "contiguous" to the text but not a part of its immanent structure. Nevertheless, without it, the text cannot produce significance nor can the analyst show how that significance is "disseminated." "Narrative can only receive its meaning," Barthes states toward the end of his "Introduction to the Structural Analysis of Narrative," "from the world that makes use of it" (115). It is the task of "textual analysis," then, to observe the codes -- "the set of protocols according to which the narrative is consumed" (116) -- that originates beyond the text but which make the text's production of significance possible. As we shall see, by thus transgressing the rule of immanence, Barthes returns us to the original questions posed by Forster: What is the difference between fictional characters and real people? How do writers of narrative deal with the tension between the demands of mimesis and the requirements of narrative structure?

In his analysis of Balzac's "Sarrasine," Barthes identifies five codes "under which all the textual signifiers can be grouped": 1) the hermeneutic code, 2) the code of semes, 3) the symbolic code, 4) the proairetic code, and 5) the cultural code.[24] Of these, it is the code of semes that makes the analysis of characters possible. The seme, as Barthes explains it, is "a connotator of persons, places, objects, of which the signified is a character" (190). Denotatively, the seme may appear as a specific attribute, an action, a speech, or even an episode, indeed, any "particle of verbal matter" that may be subjected to a semantic transformation and thereby be made to yield an attribute. Since the semes are scattered along the syntagmatic axis of narrative discourse, however, they "appear to float freely, to form a galaxy of trifling data in which we read no particular order of significance" (22). Only when the reader begins to add up the individual semes do they begin to "coalesce" into a character:

> When identical semes traverse the same proper name several times and appear to settle on it, a character is created. Thus, the character is a product of combinations: the combination is relatively stable (denoted by the recurrence of the semes) and more or less complex, involving more or less congruent, more or less contradictory figures; this complexity determines the character's personality, which is just as much a combination as the odor of a dish or the bouquet of a wine. (67)

While the semes and their connotative power are relatively easy to recognize, the naming of the connotations (i.e., the attributes or traits) is by no means a simple task. On the contrary, it is always "uncertain, approximate, unstable":

> The process of nomination... is the essence of the reader's activity; to read is to struggle to name, to subject the sentences of the text to a semantic transformation... This transformation is erratic, it consists of hesitating among several names. (92)

Indeed, the very term "nomination" may be somewhat misleading, for as Barthes says later, "the connotator refers not so much to a name, as a synonymic complex whose common nucleus we sense, even while the discourse is leading us toward other possibilities, toward other related signifiers" (92). But whether the reader actively and consciously names the connotations as he progresses through the narrative, or simply "senses" the existence of a "synonymic complex," the individual semes cannot be fully analyzed, nor can a character fully emerge, until the entire set of semes is considered as a whole. Thus, the process of reading in general, and the "reading" of characters in particular, involves what Barthes calls a "metonymic skid." Signification must be constantly posited, reviewed, and revised as new semes make their appearance.

What finally enables us to "add up" all the possibilities of meaning and to organize them into a coherent system is the Proper Name. "The name is an instrument of exchange: it allows a substitution of a nominal unit for a collection of characteristics by establishing an equivalent relationship between sign and sum..." (95). Indeed, the power of the Proper Name is such that it promotes the illusion that the character is somehow more than the sum of his attributes, that he exists beyond the semes that constitute him.

This illusion, however, depends upon more than the "economic" relationship between the semes and the Proper Name, for what we make of this relationship, the "names" that we use to describe it, is based upon a more or less complete, more or less explicit ideology of character which we bring to our reading of the text. Now this ideology will vary from period to period and may be based upon our knowledge of literary genres as well as our knowledge of life. Recognizing its role in our analysis of characters in narrative (as opposed to using it), however, may be extremely difficult. Indeed, the ideology of character reflected in texts whose conventions are most familiar to us (Barthes' "readerly" texts) may conform so closely to our own assumptions about characters that we may not recognize it as an ideology. Rather, the work will serve to reinforce those assumptions, to convince us that they are inherently correct and based upon natural law.

A recognition of the purely "economic" nature of the relationship between semes and proper name and of the role that ideology plays in our interpretation of that relationship forms the basis of Barthes' analysis of the characters in "Sarrasine." Barthes' goal, however, is not simply to provide semic catalogues for each character: "To inventory the semes in a classic text... is merely to observe the ideology" (190). Rather, Barthes will show how the needs of narrative discourse influence and at times dictate a character's semic portrait, so much so that the operative ideology of character may be distorted or even subverted. Thus, Barthes, in effect, takes up where Forster left off in his analysis of the struggle between the "mutinous" characters of fiction and the author's attempts to make them conform to the "main scheme of the book." Moreover, Barthes' approach to this struggle is clearly that of a Structuralist in the best sense of the term:

the narrative personage is neither "taken off the page" nor reduced to a function or by-product of one element of the overall narrative structure. Rather, the narrative personage is analyzed as a "participant" in the narrative structure with a "systematics" of its own which must, nevertheless, interact with the other participants in that structure and conform to the laws governing the structure as a whole.

The relation between character and plot is, according to Barthes, a paradoxical one. A character's action may be analyzed in terms of this semic protrait and such an analysis might yield psychological motivation and a sense of the character's freedom of action. On the other hand, the character's action may be a necessary element of the proairetic code (i.e., the plot) and thus one that the character is required to perform if the story is to continue. For example, when Sarrasine decides, against the warnings of a stranger, to keep his rendezvous with La Zambinella, one can easily attribute this decision to the set of connoted traits -- passion, obstinacy, etc. -- which earlier semes have revealed to us. As a result, Sarrasine's decision appears both psychologically consistent and an expression of his individuality. From the point of view of the plot, however, Sarrasine has no choice but to keep the rendezvous, for had he not, the story would have come to a premature end. "Sarrasine is forced by the discourse to keep his rendezvous with La Zambinella: the character's freedom is dominated by the discourse's instinct for preservation" (135).

The same paradox applies when Sarrasine later interrupts La Zambinella before she can reveal the truth about "her" sexual status. Here again, if we have a "realistic view of character," we will have no difficulty explaining the interruption in terms of Sarrasine's personality. However, "if we have a realistic view of discourse," Barthes insists, "if we consider the story being told as a mechanism which must function until the end, we will say that since the law of narrative decrees that it continue, it was necessary that the word <u>castrato</u> not be spoken" (178). Barthes' point here is that both views are correct and, indeed, "support" each other. It is precisely the "undecidability" between the two that is, according to Barthes, the mark of good "classical" narrative.

It appears, however, that classical narrative can accept a certain degree of "decidability" in the relation between character and theme. Some characters, particularly minor or secondary characters, may appear in the narrative only to contribute to thematic or symbolic patterns while the attributes ascribed to them conform to no ideology of character, psychological or otherwise. Barthes suggests that we refer to such narrative personages as "figures" since, unlike true "characters," they cannot be analyzed in terms of "biography, psychology, or time." And since their attributes derive their significance through their correlation with other elements of the symbolic code, what appear to be semes are, in reality, elements of that code. Thus, the figure is an "illegal, impersonal, anachronistic configuration of symbolic relationships."

The tension between characters and theme, then, manifests itself in the degree to which a particular narrative personage may be seen as a "character" or a "figure." Some personages may be "pure" figures, that is, their appearance in the narrative may be dictated wholly by symbolic or thematic concerns. Other personages may serve only a minor thematic function, or none at all, and thus our chief interest will be in their semic portrait. More commonly, especially in the case of major characters, "character" and "figure" will overlap and thus, as in the relationship between character and plot, the two "circuits" will remain undecidable. In such cases, our mode of analysis -- semic or symbolic -- may well depend upon what we are looking for: psychological "realism" or thematic patterns.

Marianina and Filippo, the children of Mme. and Count de Lanty in "Sarrasine," provide us with examples of "pure" figures. The two appear in the first part of the story and then are never heard from or of again. They play no part in the plot of the novella (they may be omitted without disturbing its coherence), and their semic portraits are extremely limited. To use Forster's term, they are "flat" characters. The one attribute that is ascribed to both, with considerable emphasis, is their extreme, indeed exaggerated, femininity. Now since this attribute does not coalesce with other connoted attributes to form a more or less fully developed personality (the very brevity of their appearance in the story would seem to preclude this), Barthes places the connotators of this femininity in the Symbolic Code. The children's feminity, Barthes explains, embodies "a kind of explosion of Zambinellian femininity," and thus links up with the thematic configuration that he calls the "woman's camp" or the "camp of castration" (37-38).

Now were we to analyze the children only in terms of their semic portrait, i.e., as "characters," we would be hard pressed to explain the purpose of their appearance in the tale. Indeed, we might have to conclude that Balzac is merely "padding" the tale, or, at best, attempting to populate the soirée with which the tale begins with interesting but otherwise irrelevant "types." Analyzed as "figures," on the other hand, the purpose of the children's appearance, their function in the tale, is quite clear, as are the reasons for the "flatness" of their characterization.

Because figures are, from the point of view of psychological consistency or depth, "illegal," their semic portraits can be quite fluid, indeed, subject to sudden "mutations." "As a figure, the character can oscillate between two roles, without this oscillation having any meaning, for it occurs outside of biographical time..." (68). The young woman to whom the narrator tells the story of Sarrasine, for example, oscillates between two roles in just this manner, and, as a result, transgresses the ideology of character that requires psychological consistency. In her first appearance in the novella (lexias #60, 62), she is presented as a "child-woman, transparent, fragile, fresh." Later, however, she shall appear "fully drawn, outgoing rather than receptive, in short active," a kind of "queen-woman" (beginning with lexia #90 and developed in lexias #119, 139, 142, etc.).[25] This "mutation," Barthes argues, has nothing to do with psychology; rather, it is to be explained by the "purely paradigmatic needs" of the central symbolic structure of the tale, namely, antithesis. Thus, in lexia #60, a fresh, young woman, "frail and floreal," was required to provide an antithesis to the "petrified old man" (La Zambinella). In lexia #90, on the other hand, the antithesis required "a powerful vegetality that reassembles, that unites," to oppose La Zambinella who at this point is described as a "human wreckage" (63).

While the young woman will, for a short time, oscillate between these two roles (in lexia #93 she is again presented as a "child-woman," pressing against the narrator for protection), her role as "queen-woman" will ultimately prevail until she becomes a full-fledged member of the active, powerful, domineering camp of castration. And it is as such that she symbolically condemns the narrator, who has meanwhile mutated from powerful protector to "dominated subject," to Sarrasine's fate (63).

In the case of at least secondary characters, then, it appears that a classically realistic text can withstand certain transgressions against an ideology of character that demands, among other things, psychological consistency. We are prepared to accept characters who fail to conform to this ideology or who even subvert it if, as "figures," they can be integrated into a symbolic or thematic structure. But is this also the case with regard to the main characters who command our attention throughout the narrative and are thus subject to a more careful, more demanding scrutiny than characters who make their limited appearance and then fade into the shadows?

From the example of "Sarrasine," it would appear that the classically realistic text must maintain a certain equilibrium between the demand for "realistic" characterization of the protagonist -- in this case Sarrasine -- and the needs of the discourse. We have already noted, for example, the "undecidability" involved in the relation between the discourse's "instinct for preservation" and our ability (abetted by the discourse itself) to interpret Sarrasine's actions in terms of a psychologically coherent semic portrait. We may note, additionally, the great stability of that portrait: attributes connoted from the story of his youth -- violence (lexia #177), femininity (lexia #158), impiety (lexia #162), obstinacy (lexia #169) -- reappear and indeed play a key role in later events (see, for example, lexias #430, 302, 379, 412). What this indicates, of course, is that Sarrasine is, in Barthes' terms, clearly a "character."

Still, Barthes insists that we can make a distinction between Sarrasine's "character" and his "figure," between, in other words, the illusion of his individuality created by the stability of his semic portrait and the ability of those semes to function as elements of other codes.

> Occasionally we speak of Sarrasine as though he existed, as though he had a future, an unconscious, a soul. However, what we are talking about is his figure (an impersonal network of symbols combined under the Proper Name), not his person (a moral freedom endowed with motives and an overdetermination of meaning): we are developing connotations, not pursuing investigations, searching for a systematics of a (transitory) site in the text (marked under the name of Sarrasine)... (92)

Thus, even with characters who conform to an ideology of character and about whom we can speak as though they "existed," we cannot limit ourselves to the cataloguing and analysis of their semes. For while such an analysis may yield the illusion of "a moral freedom endowed with motives," seen from a different perspective the semes may also form an "impersonal network of symbols," the elements of which derive their significance from their correlation with other elements of the symbolic code. As in the case of actions, then, the attributes of a "character" can belong to various circuits, can function as elements in various codes. If our goal is to discover a "systematics" underlying the relationship between a proper name and the semantic units attached to it -- if, in other words, the object of our analysis is the narrative personage and not simply the "person" -- no circuit can be ignored.

Barthes' analysis of the narrative personages -- "characters" and "figures" -- in "Sarrasine," then, confirms or is at least in accord with Forster's insight into the fundamental tension involved in the creation of fictional characters. Forster, we will recall, viewed characters as "creations within a creation" who, for all their "parallels with people like ourselves," must ultimately conform to the "main scheme of the book" in which they appear. Similarly, Barthes shows that narrative personages serve, as it were, two masters: an ideology of character external to the narrative, and the narrative discourse itself with its own needs and requirements. This tension, both Forster and Barthes observe, can be resolved in favor of the discourse by the creation of narrative personages -- "flat characters" or "figures" -- who fail to conform to our notions about real people but who perform important plot or thematic functions. More often, however (at least in classically realistic narrative), the tension will remain in a state of equilibrium. Thus Sarrasine, certainly a "round character" by Forster's definition, keeps his rendezvous with La Zambinella because he is passionate, but he is passionate because the plot and theme of the novella require a passionate protagonist. The "circuits," Barthes reminds us, are "undecidable" -- an indication of the inherent plurality of the "galaxy of signifiers" of which the narrative is composed.

This leads us, however, to methodological questions concerning Barthes' organization of the narrative's signifiers into codes. For if the signifiers of narrative are inherently "plural" -- that is, if they may function as elements of various circuits or codes -- assigning them to specific codes surely violates this plurality. To place the connotators of Sarrasine's passion in the code of semes, for example, when they also function as elements in an "impersonal network of symbols" (i.e., the symbolic code), or to place actions occasioned by Sarrasine's passion in the proairetic code when they also obviously contribute to his semic portrait, is nothing less than an attempt to decide the "undecidable."

Barthes, it is true, argues that a classically realistic text such as "Sarrasine" is only "moderately plural." Yet his insistence upon assigning each and every semantic unit to a specific code, often in what appears to be a rather arbitrary manner, violates even this moderate plurality, and certainly the absolute plurality of Barthes' "ideal text":

> In this ideal text, the networks are many and interact, without any one of them being able to surpass the rest; this text is a galaxy of signifiers, not a structure of signifieds; it has no beginning; it is reversible; we gain access to it by several entrances, none of which can be authoritatively declared the main one... (5)

Barthes' codes violate the moderate plurality of "Sarrasine" by establishing a set of hierarchies that contradict or at least blur the essential reversibility of its semantic units, by declaring, in effect, that some "networks," at least locally, "surpass the rest."

Barthes' "textual analysis" of "Sarrasine" differs from the practice of other Structuralists and, indeed, from his own practice in his "Introduction to the Structural Analysis of Narrative," in two important ways. First, he eschews the attempt to apply linguistic models in toto -- deep structure, traditional syntax, levels of description, etc. -- to the analysis of narrative discourse. Second, he ignores the "rule of immanence" of structural analysis by basing his analysis upon semiotic systems -- "codes" -- that extend beyond the text itself. Indeed, his statement that all codes are, ultimately, cultural (18) leads one to the inescapable conclusion that without a knowledge of "culture" the text would be unintelligible. One may well argue that it is precisely these differences which lead Barthes to emphasize the "plurality" of the text and to call for an open-ended, non-hierarchical reading of the "galaxy of signifiers" with which the text confronts us. Still, whether because of his ideological commitment to certain Structuralist positions (e.g., the rejection of language as representation), or because he is encumbered by an ill-chosen system of notation (the "starred text"), Barthes ultimately fails to "open-up" the text as completely as he himself appears to desire.

In his attempt to develop a "unified theory of the literary text," on the other hand, Benjamin Hrushovski avoids these pitfalls and, as a result, provides us with a conceptual model that more adequately describes the "plurality" with which Barthes unsuccessfully grapples. It will be worth our while to trace the main elements of Hrushovski's "unified theory," for it goes a long way toward solving many of the problems relating to characters and their attributes that have been raised in our analysis of the more "main stream" Structuralists.

Hrushovski draws upon linguistics and semiotics in developing his theory but, like Barthes (at least in S/Z), he rejects the notion that one can mechanically apply linguistic models to narrative discourse. Instead he focuses upon the unfolding "text continuum" which, he states, "has its own logic and its own organization from which the reader is led to construct both 'form' and 'meaning,' plot, style, structure, ideas, world view, and genre properties, and so on."[26] Thus, Hrushovski's "unified theory" takes into account the intrinsic properties of the text itself (its "logic" and "organization") as well as the active role of the reader in "realizing" the "possible or plausible" patterns embedded in the text.

This process of "realization" is accomplished by the reader's "linking up" the numerous semantic and non-semantic units dispersed along the text continuum. "A text," Hrushovski states, "is a highly complex network of patterns of all kinds... we link up dispersed elements in the text in order to construct plot, character A and character B, the writer's point of view of peasant society, style, parallelism of various kinds, etc." (4). Now there are, according to Hrushovski, at least three principles of "pattern construction." First, elements may be linked up according to a principle of equivalence. Thus in poetry, for example, we link up repeated sounds in order to "realize" alliteration and rhyme. Secondly, pattern construction may be based upon "reality-like principles." We may link up the attributes of a certain persona or character, for example, according to extraliterary notions of psychology. Finally, pattern construction may be based upon a combination of the first two principles, for example, according to our recognition of certain generic properties.

Now for our purposes, the second principle described by Hrushovski is especially significant, for it introduces the principle of mimesis as a possible basis for realizing elements of the literary text. "We not only use literature to understand the world," Hrushovski maintains, "but we use the world, as well as all possible worlds, to understand and construct literary texts" (4). As we have seen, it is this very aspect of reading that the Structuralists, both for ideological and methodological reasons, have attempted to ignore, or at least remove from their analysis of the immanent structure of narrative, and which Barthes attempted to deal with by declaring his intention to "transgress" the "rule of immanence." For Hrushovski, on the other hand, no pattern (with the exception, perhaps, of those composed purely of non-semantic elements, e.g., sound patterns) is any more or less immanent. Our ability to realize and construct patterns, be they patterns of plot, theme, character, or setting, is always dependent, at least in part, upon our knowledge of the world. It follows, then, that there can be no privileged material for the structural analysis of literary texts based upon the criterion of immanence.

But Hrushovski goes even farther. Neither the structure of the various patterns nor the process through which the reader realizes them differs from pattern to pattern. In each case, the reader will have to "scan" the whole text, gather together the diverse elements, and construct a pattern on the basis of one or another principle of construction. Moreover, any pattern may be composed of homogeneous as well as heterogeneous material. Thus, for example, the elements of the reconstructed plot may be derived from explicit event statements as well as from "extrinsic" non-event elements such as dialogue, character description, mood, etc. Similarly, a character pattern may be based upon material "proper" to that pattern -- explicit attributes, for example -- as well as "extrinsic" event statements.

Hrushovski, then, is in apparent agreement with Barthes who, we will recall, pointed out that any "particle of verbal material" can be subjected to a semantic transformation and thus be made part of the Code of Semes. Indeed, Hrushovski's description of the process of the realization of patterns through linking up diverse elements in the narrative parallels Barthes' description of reading as a "metonymic skid" in which signifiers are named according to observed correlations. It is in the naming of the semantic units, however, that Hrushovski differs significantly from Barthes. We have argued that Barthes' practice of identifying each semantic unit by reference to one specific code is a major weakness in his methodology, for it tends to obscure the essential plurality or reversibility of the semantic units and, moreover, to establish the kind of hierarchical reading that Barthes himself clearly rejects. Hrushovski avoids these difficulties by referring to the semantic units as "junctions," a term that places proper emphasis upon the unit's ability to "fit into" or "contribute" to several patterns simultaneously. Thus, even a "proper" event statement is not "named" solely in terms of its participation, however essential, in the plot pattern. For just as there is no "pure event material" in language, there can be no "pure" event in narrative:

> Each passage of a text presenting an event has to contribute at the same time to a number of other patterns: the characters participating in the event, the

setting in which the event occurs, etc. Such a passage is, clearly, a <u>junction</u> in which several heterogeneous patterns meet, intersect, and interact (though one of them may be dominant). (8)

The same thing is true, we might add, of characters' attributes. There can be no "pure" attribute (or seme), for, by the very nature of the literary text, it must contribute not only to a character pattern but to various other patterns as well.

It is true, however, that one of the patterns intersecting the junction "may be dominant." Indeed, Hrushovski points out that "the patterns of a text create a complex network of hierarchies" without which we could not "grasp" large and complex works of literature. But these hierarchies, Hrushovski insists, are not "stable and architectonic":

> In order for the reader to realize properly a certain point in the development of the plot or create the correct tension at this point, it is not enough that he simply links up the events which lead up to this point. He must construct the characters or the persons involved in the event, the social and moral norms which regulate their behavior, etc. In this case, such patterns as character or norms of behavior are <u>subordinated</u> to a single point in the pattern of plot. But at a later stage we may wish to construct a certain character and then an abstraction from the whole plot in which the character participated may be subordinated to a conclusion about this character. (6)

The variety of patterns to which the semantic units of narrative can contribute, and the fact that at any point one pattern may be subordinated to another -- on the basis of local requirements of the text or "the interests of the reader at the moment" -- are, according to Hrushovski, "very characteristic feature(s) of literary texts" (6).

What Hrushovski has done, then, is to integrate characters and their attributes, as one pattern among others, into the global structure of the narrative in which they appear. The character pattern, to be sure, can be subordinated to other patterns, but this subordination must never be mistaken for a "stable and architectonic" element of the narrative. To reduce the character to the rule of "actor" or "agent of action," for example, not only wrenches the character from the network of patterns, but does so at the cost of ignoring other patterns to which the character may contribute and which may be of equal or greater importance than the pattern of plot. For, as Hrushovski argues, a character's actions not only serve as "homogeneous" elements of the plot pattern, they may also contribute to other patterns in the text, such as theme, symbolic configurations, ideas, and, of course, the character pattern itself. The character may be seen, then, as a kind of nexus in which various patterns "meet, intersect, and interact," and the kind of "character analysis" Hrushovski's model seems to call for would be an analysis of the extent and nature of those intersections.

Benjamin Hrushovski's (and the later Roland Barthes') most important contribution to the Structuralist tradition, then, has to do with the question of hierarchy. Following the lead of the Russian Formalists, earlier Structuralists identified action or incident as the fundamental narrative unit. As a result, narrative discourse was analyzed only in terms of the syntagmatic organization of terms denoting action, and all other patterns in the text were subordinated to this pattern. Characters were reduced to "agents of action" while their attributes fell out of the structure altogether. One could get the impression that characters represented for the Structuralists a kind of necessary evil required to get the "real" job of narrative accomplished, namely, telling a story.

But this hierarchical approach to narrative discourse conforms neither to the way we read literary texts, at least as Barthes and Hrushovski describe it, nor to the data. Todorov, for example, recognized a "trend" in narrative in which actions are "a means of access to the personality in question, if not a symptom," but chose not to analyze such narratives for the sake of "rigor." And Barthes' notion of "indices" (developed in his essay, "Introduction to Structural Analysis of Narratives") allowed him to distinguish between "heavily functional" and "heavily indicial" narratives as well as a whole class of "intermediary" forms, yet he abandoned "pure" structural analysis in S/Z in order to deal with such "mixed" narratives. Now if the "rigor" of one's analysis prevents one from dealing effectively with a large and significant body of texts, then it is perhaps not a question of rigor at all, but of flawed assumption about the essential nature of the material under analysis.

The flaw in the assumptions of the earlier Structuralists, I would argue, may be traced to their dismissal of the mimetic aspect of narrative discourse, their refusal to allow for the fact that, as Hrushovski argues, "we use the world, as well as all possible worlds, to understand and construct literary texts." Whether this refusal stems from their pursuit of analogies between literature and linguistics, their concern with methodological rigor, or their polemical stance against naive notions of realism and verisimilitude, the Structuralists clearly erred in their extremism. To be sure, conventions of verisimilitude, as the Structuralists never tire of pointing out, are bound to specific periods and genres, and only a hopelessly parochial point of view would equate the conventions of nineteenth-century fiction with some universal standard of realism. Yet, as Robert Alter has argued, "it is by no means clear why the choice of details in a fictional narrative cannot be dictated simultaneously by principles of internal coherence and by the writer's sense of a just, plausible correspondence to the social, moral, psychological facts of real existence as he understands them."[27] Thus, in works in which conventions of verisimilitude are operative, if only as one motivating factor among others in an author's choice and organization of detail, they must be accounted for if one's analysis is to have any relevance to the structure it purports to describe.

* * *

In the chapters that follow, I shall analyze four novels by three modern Hebrew novelists in regard to the protagonists that appear in them. It is not my intention, however, to subordinate all other elements or patterns in the novels under consideration to the analysis or "realization" of their protagonists, nor to propose an alternative hierarchy to that according to which only actions constitute the fundamental narrative unit. Rather, I shall attempt to analyze the complex relationship between the protagonist and, to use Forster's term, "the main scheme" of the work in which he appears. Specifically, I hope to show how various narrative elements -- plot, theme, symbolic and ideational configurations -- both individually and in concert, influence and at times dictate modes and techniques of character construction. I shall not, on the other hand, ignore the role that the mimetic intentions of the authors in question play in the construction of their protagonists. Indeed, it is precisely the tension between mimesis -- whether based upon a certain ideology of human behavior, or other "reality-like" principles -- and the "requirements" of narrative discourse that shall be one of our main concerns.

In dealing with these issues, I shall not systematically apply one or any combination of the models of structural analysis of narrative that we have discussed, nor shall I attempt to construct and apply a model of my own. Rather, my approach will be inductive, as far as this is possible. Through a close reading of each novel, treating the analysis of the protagonist as a point of entry rather than a goal in itself, I shall attempt to shed some light on the complex nature of the relationship between protagonist, as "participant" in a narrative structure, and the other elements of that structure, and I shall try, moreover, to indicate the variety of ways in which that relationship can be pursued.

I shall, to be sure, have occasion to refer to and at times apply to my own analysis elements of structural analysis (both "pure" and "impure"), but such application will be dictated by my inductive approach. My criterion will be the extent to which the principles or insights of structural analysis prove useful or particularly illuminating in regard to specific "problems" in the texts under consideration. Finally, I shall reserve my conclusions concerning a general poetics of literary character for a separate chapter. Such conclusions, needless to say, will be derived directly from our experience in analyzing the novels I have chosen to consider.

CHAPTER THREE
Mendele in Pieces: S.Y. Abramovitsh's
The Beggars' Book

At that moment, my body stretches itself out and becomes very light, like a thing of no substance. Mendele breaks up into little pieces, and those pieces spin and flutter about in the air so that one cannot tell where the center is or what piece is the main piece. Suddenly I have two faces and two Mendeles jostle each other... "Good evening," says one Mendele with a bow, "where are you off to on a night like this?"[1]

Having completed a day of fasting, as required of Jews on the 17th of Tammuz, Mendele, the narrator-hero of S.Y. Abramovitsh's The Beggars' Book, fortifies himself with a drink of wine before setting off in search of his friend, Reb Alter Yaknehoz. On an empty stomach, the wine has immediate and powerful effect, and the hallucination of Mendele in Pieces is the result. In the dialogue between the two Mendeles that eventually emerge from the pieces, one Mendele indulges in tears of self-pity, invoking the hardships and humiliations he must suffer as a Jew. The other Mendele merely scoffs, telling his tearful other half to get on with the search. "Quiet down! A Jew should complain? A grown-up Jew with a wife and children stands and bawls to the moon in the middle of the night and isn't ashamed of himself? Hold your tears and be still... the devil won't carry you off... [H103; Y52].

Mendele seems to be a man in serious conflict with himself, the victim of an identity crisis of no small proportions. At least that is what, as post-Freudian readers, we would assume to be the symbolic import of the hallucination and its "dream-work." But if this is an identity crisis, it is a curiously short-lived one. After the brief dialogue, the "pieces" are quickly reassembled and Mendele returns to his narrative duties as if nothing had transpired. He does not pause to consider the implications of his hallucination, nor does he suffer a similar breakdown in The Beggars' Book.[2] The conflict, moreover, plays no part in the plot of the novel and its psychological implications are neither developed nor explored. Indeed, the quasi-allegorical terms in which Abramovitsh evokes the inner conflict of his protagonist discourages this kind of development. By personifying the conflicting impulses as two autonomous and antagonistic Mendeles, he leaves himself little room in which to reunite them, to show how they can co-exist in a single psychological configuration. Rather, Mendele simply and suddenly deconstructs and then, just as suddenly, comes back together again. But for that isolated moment, Mendele becomes an enigma both to himself and to us: "...one cannot tell where the center is or which piece is the main piece."

The critics, of course, have ignored Mendele's warning. Indeed, the question of Mendele's true identity -- the "main piece" -- has preoccupied Hebrew and Yiddish literary critics from Abramovitsh's day to our own, and the efforts have led to widely varying results. Mendele has been described as the most Jewish of Jews, a folk-type symbolizing the Jewish people, a man with a tragic vision, a humanist and apostate essentially alienated from his Jewish environment, and even an anti-semite.[3] Efforts at identifying Mendele were considerably complicated, moreover, by the fact that, early in his career, Abramovitsh adopted the name of his main character and narrator as his pseudonym. As a result, critics often confused the issue by equating the fictional character with the author himself.[4]

Mendele's enigmatic quality, then, is not confined to isolated moments of deconstruction. The "main piece" has consistently eluded the critics, and claims of having discovered it have invariably evoked heated counter-claims. Few critics, however, would find much to quarrel with in Dan Miron's estimation of Mendele as "one of the best, most lively, and round characters ever created by a Jewish writer of fiction."[5] Nor, I suspect, would Gershon Shaked's statement that there are only two characters in Abramovitsh's fictional world -- Mendele and the collectivity of Am Yisrael -- evoke much debate.[6]

Now the paradoxical situation of a "memorable" character who evokes different and at times widely diverging memories is certainly not an unprecedented phenomenon. From Odysseus to Leopold Bloom, fictional characters have been made the object of countless "character sketches," ranging from impressionistic and personal responses to sophisticated analyses based upon the psychological or psycho-sociological theories in vogue at any given moment. It is little wonder, then, that the results of these efforts have often varied. Still, a case such as Mendele, in which the responses have varied so widely and evoked so much controversy in a relatively short span of time, presents us with an interesting opportunity to consider the source and the implications of this paradox.

One of the assumptions shared by the critics whose views on Mendele I have cited is that fictional characters can and indeed should be analyzed as though they were real people. They speak, for example, of Mendele's personality, of some psychological essence underlying and explaining his overt speech and behavior, they speculate as to Mendele's values and motives, and they may even attempt to explain these in terms of Mendele's past or present biographical situation. As we saw in the previous chapter, however, the analysis of fictional characters as though they were real people has come under considerable suspicion in recent years. Rather than analyzing characters as more or less accurate representations of human beings as we know them or believe we know them, the Structuralists we considered insist upon treating fictional characters as constructs, as functioning elements in a narrative structure, and their goal is to define the nature of that function.

At the outset, at least, we will follow the advice of the Structuralists and view Mendele not as a "being" but as a "participant." Thus, rather than attempting to reassemble the pieces revealed in Mendele's hallucination and to identify or name the "main piece," a task which, as we have seen, has evoked more controversy than concensus, we will attempt to define Mendele's function in the narrative structure and then show how the requirements of that structure affect and largely determine Mendele's semic portrait.

Although his precise role varies considerably, Mendele appears in most of Abramovitsh's major works. At times, he is a fictional editor who provides an introduction or epilogue to the documents he has "received." His editorial role, however, may lead him to make substantial changes in the "original" text and when this happens he becomes, in effect, the narrator of the "improved" tale. In other works, he describes events that he himself has witnessed, and in a few cases he emerges as a full-fledged character, a narrator-hero who not only reports on the action but plays a major role in it. Regardless of his varying visibility, however, Mendele's structural function remains constant: He is the intermediary between the reader and Jewish society and it is only through him that, ultimately, the reader has access to that society. Dan Miron has put it succinctly: Whenever Mendele speaks, it is "his consciousness that constitutes the fictional world."[7]

In The Beggars' Book, Abramovitsh exploits Mendele's role as intermediary more fully and consistently than in any other work. Here he is both narrator and actor and, at least in the first thirteen chapters of the novel, he remains steadily in the foreground. The events that form the object of Mendele's narrative consist largely of his encounters on the road with fellow Jews and the swapping of tales which, in Mendele's world, invariably follows from such encounters. Thus, when Mendele meets up with Reb Alter Yaknehoz, an itinerent book peddler like himself, the latter tells Mendele of his recent misadventure at a nearby fair where, in his eagerness to earn a commission, he mistakenly made a "match" between two young men. Mendele, in turn, tells Reb Alter of Fishke, a crippled bathhouse attendant who obtained a bride when, in their eagerness not to lose their commission (and the pleasures of a marriage feast), the matchmakers and other town "officials" chose him as a last-minute substitute for an unwilling groom. After a night searching for their horses, which had wandered off into a nearby forest while they were talking, Mendele and Reb Alter resume their tale swapping, this time with the participation of a third party. Reb Alter tells Mendele how, in the course of the night, he saved their horses from a band of roving beggars and discovered a miserable beggar left for dead in an abandoned hovel. When Mendele recognizes that the beggar is none other than Fishke, the subject of his earlier tale, both Mendele and Reb Alter urge the new arrival to tell his story. In his tale (which takes up more than half of the novel), Fishke describes the disastrous consequences of his unexpected marriage and the grief-filled chain of events that led him to the hovel in which Reb Alter discovered him. After all the tales are told, Reb Alter declares that the hunchbacked waif with whom Fishke found solace during his torments is none other than the daughter whom he had abandoned years before. Moved by Fishke's description of her miseries, Reb Alter sets off to find her and make up for his past misdeeds. Mendele and Fishke continue with heavy hearts on the road to Kisalon.

Although Mendele participates in the action of The Beggars' Book on an equal footing with the other characters and converses with them as one Jew to another, as narrator and intermediary he is in a uniquely privileged position. He is the only character to whom the reader has direct access -- all the others are known to us only through Mendele's description and commentary. And he is the only character who can address the reader directly -- for the others the reader simply does not exist. Indeed Mendele is guilty of a certain duplicity or, at the very least, a conflict of loyalties. For even as he accepts the confidences of the other characters, seemingly sharing their values and concerns, he does not hesitate to go behind their backs, as it were, and hold their values and behavior up to ridicule before the reader. But Mendele is in fact guilty of more than duplicity; he is also guilty of defying the laws of nature. For as narrator and intermediary, he succeeds in being in two places at one time: in the "world" of <u>The Beggars' Book</u> (the world inhabited by Reb Alter and Fishke), and in the "world" of the reader. Mendele's privileged position, then, is uniquely literary; there is no analogy to it in real life where we are all confined, for the time being at least, to one world.

Mendele moves from one world to the other almost constantly and with absolute ease. Even as he participates in the action or listens to a tale he may at any moment absent himself from the immediate situation and turn, as it were, directly to the reader. When, for example, Mendele and Reb Alter meet on the road to Kisalon, Mendele tells us that they immediately begin to question each other "in the manner of Jews," and when Reb Alter responds to Mendele's questions, he does so, Mendele points out, "according to Jewish practice in which one does not respond properly with a straightforward answer but rather acquits oneself with a grimace and a grunt" [H92; Y14]. Later, when Mendele attempts to get the unresponsive Reb Alter to tell his tale, he turns to the subject of business since, as he explains to the reader, "there is no better ruse than that to get a Jew talking" [H94; Y22].

These little asides to the reader often expand into long comic digressions in which Mendele speaks of Jewish behavior in general. Thus, after his ruse takes effect and Reb Alter begins his tale, Mendele once more turns to the reader and explains why it worked so well: "Even when a Jew is dying, as soon as he hears of business matters his mind immediately settles down and the angel of death, taken aback, loses control of the situation. Too bad for anyone who visits a Jewish merchant when his mind is set on business! At that instant, the whole world doesn't mean a thing to him and he dismisses his best friend and even his own brother with a mere glance. But that's not my point" [H94; Y22]. Reb Alter's predictable response to Mendele's manipulation serves as the catalyst for a satiric commentary upon Jewish society and its mores. While Reb Alter is reduced to caricature, his behavior is seen as typical rather than eccentric, symptomatic of a society which, in Mendele's view, has made business its supreme value. Indeed, it almost seems as if Mendele's encounter with Reb Alter and his manipulation of the Jewish "business ethic" are merely pretexts for pushing his satiric message, for exposing to the reader this ludicrous element of Jewish behavior.[8]

But Mendele does not have to interrupt the action by turning to the reader in order to push his satiric message. Even when he speaks to the other characters, it is often the reader who is the real addressee. When, for example, Mendele expresses amazement at Reb Alter's blunder at the fair and asks him how he could have fallen into such a trap, Reb Alter is surprised at Mendele's sudden ignorance. "Were anyone to hear you they might mistakenly think that 'his honor' is not a Jew at all, heaven forbid, and does not know how matches are made... It seems to me, Reb Mendele, that you certainly do know the customs of the Jews and the way we handle marriage arrangements" [H96; Y27]. Reb Alter is quite justified in reacting in this manner, for he does not know (and cannot know) that Mendele does not ask his question for his own enlightenment but rather for that of the reader. Mendele's loyalty to the reader and his habit of using his encounters on the road to illustrate aspects of his satiric message result in a temporary breakdown in communication with Reb Alter. Unaware of Mendele's hidden purpose, Reb Alter finds his behavior inexplicable.

A similar breakdown in communication occurs in Mendele's story about Fishke. When Mendele launches into a detailed and mockingly elegiac description of the Jewish bathhouse, Reb Alter cannot understand why Mendele must interrupt his story with such useless information. "What's he talking about? A bathhouse? So what's the point? Bless the Lord, I have seen many a bathhouse in my day..." [H99; Y37].[9] Once again, Reb Alter's complaint is perfectly justified. He has indeed seen many bathhouses and thus is in no need of Mendele's description. Mendele lingers over his description, of course, not for Reb Alter's benefit, even though he is the apparent addressee, but for the benefit of the reader. The satiric intent of the description, of course, goes completely over Reb Alter's head.

When Mendele does address the reader, he often ends up apologizing for his "digressions" by protesting that "that's not my point." This narrative sweep of the hand emphasizes the "told" nature of the narrative as well as Mendele's role as intermediary between Jewish society and the reader. Indeed, Mendele's apparent inability to stick to the point gives his narrative the quality of a verbal improvisation, as if we were dealing with a narrator who is not quite in control of his narrative and is constantly getting side-tracked by his own verbosity. Abramovitsh inherited this technique from the Russian skaz, a conversational narrative style that thrives upon digressions and narrative faux pas for its comic effects. Like the narrators of Gogol's stories, Mendele's familiar conversational style, his constant asides to the reader, and his frequent digressions foreground the narrative at the expense of what is narrated. We are, in the end, less interested in what happens than in what Mendele has to say about what happens.[10]

Mendele's comic manipulation of biblical and rabbinical allusions plays a major role in the foregrounding of the narrative. Wrenching phrases from their original context, Mendele employs them, sometimes with slight but crucial modifications, to describe entirely mundane and even trivial matters. In the new context, the elevated connotations of the phrase are subverted or completely reversed; the spiritual is reduced to the grossly physical, the sacred suddenly appears profane. At the same time, the new context itself receives a new signification. The short-circuited allusion (to borrow Baruch Kurzweil's image) emphasizes the spiritual poverty of the present which, forced to stand in the shadow of ultimate meaning, appears all the more absurd. Thus, for example, when the two book peddlers decide in the absence of cash to swap books as well as stories, Mendele uses a biblical phrase to describe Reb Alter's enthusiasm over the prospect of doing business. Reb Alter, Mendele tells us, was as happy "as one who has discovered much booty" [H101; Y44].[11] In Psalm 119, this simile captures the speaker's joy over God's promise of salvation; in the new context, the simile takes on a more literal meaning, for Reb Alter has indeed found much booty, even though he can hardly expect to gain much profit from Mendele's tattered wares. Spiritual exaltation has been replaced by exaggerated and ultimately futile economic zealousness, sacred yearnings reduced to a mechanical struggle for subsistence. In the same paragraph, Mendele is able to capture this reversal of values as well as the ultimate futility of this "business ethic" in a single phrase by slightly modifying a well-known rabbinic dictum. Both sides derived satisfaction from the transaction even though not a penny changed hands because, as Mendele puts it, "the reward of business -- is business" [H101; Y44].[12]

Through his manipulation of allusions, Mendele can transform relatively commonplace occurrences into comic situations and opportunities for satiric commentary. When, for example, some peasants who happen to pass by help Mendele and Reb Alter untangle their wagons, Mendele makes use of rabbinic gloss on a biblical verse to describe the action.[13] "They were pushing just right, and from their pushing it was clear that the hands were the hands of Esau. As for us, forgive the comparison, our strength is only in our mouth -- the voice is the voice of Jacob. And so while they pushed we yelled, push on, push on, for the voice is useful for pushing..." [H92; Y15].

While in the rabbinic tradition the biblical verse was interpreted symbolically as an expression of the eternal conflict between Jew (Jacob) and Gentile (Esau), Mendele, as in the previous example, applies the metaphor to a mundane situation and in doing so reverses its original meaning and effect. The self-flattering rabbinic distinction between the spiritual Jew and the coarse, physical Gentile turns into an indictment of the Jew's helplessness in physical matters and his abject dependency upon the Gentile to get along in life.

Mendele's short-circuited allusions are not a matter of chance or an unconscious distortion of a pious Jew's natural propensity to embellish his speech with scriptural verse and rabbinic maxims. In spite of his protests to the contrary, Mendele is in complete control of his narrative, and it is precisely in his digressions and his "reinterpretations" of traditional phrases that he makes his most telling points. It does not take long, in fact, for the reader to realize that whenever Mendele says, "But that's not my point," he means just the opposite. At one point, moreover, Mendele takes the reader into his confidence in order to justify his narrative procedures. In the process, he fashions an elaborate parody of the "mosaic" style of nineteenth-century Hebrew writers according to whom a sublime style could be achieved only by stringing together biblical verses and phrases: "A Jewish poet would have found ample material ready at hand that morning with which to write a lovely song... And, the muses willing, he might have added a few touches of his own: A flock of sheep grazing in the roses, cows grazing among the reeds, a hind longing for running streams... But we are in no need of his bag of tricks. We have, thank God, baggage of our own... As for me, I will tell what is in the depths of my heart on my own" [H111; Y77].[14] For Mendele, telling his story on his own means exploiting the comic devices of the skaz, playing the narrative game for the enjoyment of his reader and at the expense of his companions on the road. He is an irrepressible storyteller whose one abiding passion is to transform his encounters on the road into comic narrative and opportunities to push his satiric message. In typical skaz, we laugh at the narrator and his narrative clumsiness; in The Beggars' Book, we laugh with the narrator and take pleasure in his only lightly concealed narrative ingenuity.

Mendele is not, however, a consistently detached observer of Jewish life. When his attention turns to the circumstances responsible for the behavior of his comic victims he can reveal hidden stories of sympathy and understanding. On such occasions, Mendele abandons his usual conversational style and indulges in highly charged, melodramatic prose. The self-serving rhetoric of irony suddenly gives way to the effusiveness of sentimental identification and the narrative game turns serious. When, during his search for the horses, Mendele ends up in an inn run by his relative Haya-Traina and her hen-pecked husband, Haim-Hona, he describes the poverty, filth, and ignorance that he finds there from his usual detached point of view. Sympathy and sentimental rhetoric are comically shifted to a fly-bespattered portrait of Napoleon that hangs on one of the walls: "Woe to him and woe to his soul, how his face was changed! His glory has descended -- now he makes his abode in this Jewish inn..." [H106; Y61]. When he is finally left alone for the night, however, Mendele reveals some very different sentiments in his plaint to the moon:

> Oh dear Mother... the pain is so great. How afflictions are multiplied and how we suffer and grieve day after day. The eye of the envious falls even on the bread of our affliction, on the little we have to eat in wrath and worry... and as if the trouble and pain and affliction that assault the flesh were not enough, more miseries and harsh torments are heaped on by others. Even in this life of distress, which really isn't life at all but a protracted death throe, envy has the upper hand. Oh dear Mother, how bitter it is to me, how great the pain. [H108; Y66]

Mendele identifies with the Jews, making it clear that he shares both their plight (poverty, hunger, undeserved hatred) and their pain. Indeed, he shares more than that. Whenever Mendele describes his own behavior, he invariably refers to it as being no less typically Jewish than that of Reb Alter. After pouring out his heart to the moon, he tells us that "a spark of hope flickered within me like that which comes to a Jew after he has stood in prayer before the Omniscient One and has told Him all his troubles" [H108; Y66]. In fact, Mendele often uses his own behavior, just as he does that of Reb Alter, as a pretext for satiric digressions on typical Jewish behavior. After spending the night at Haya-Traina's inn, Mendele describes getting up in the morning in this manner:

> It wasn't by my own will that I got up early that morning. My limbs weighed me down from the bumps of the road, but necessity pushed me out of bed and set me on my feet. The Jew lives and moves on momentum alone. In action and speech, in bargaining and all his deeds, he is always in a rush, always pressed for time. But if the momentum begins to weaken a bit, his body is immediately enfeebled and he collapses like a golem. [H108; Y67]

No longer a detached observer criticizing and ridiculing the behavior of others, Mendele has become both the observed and the observer, the object of his own satirical scorn.

Mendele's privileged position -- his ability to be in two "worlds" at the same time -- allows him, indeed, requires him to be both an "everyday" Jew and a detached observer of everyday Jewish behavior, including his own. Among his companions on the road, Mendele may at times act oddly, but he is clearly a Jew among Jews, trapped by the same social and economic circumstances that trap all Jews and, when pressed, responding to those circumstances with the same stereotypical patterns of behavior. When Mendele turns to the reader, on the other hand, his values and attitudes undergo a radical reorientation and he is able to observe and analyze Jewish behavior -- including his own -- from a perspective that his companions on the road would have a difficult time understanding, much less sharing. It is this apparent split in Mendele's narrative personality that has been the source of much of the confusion over his "identity." Critics who chose to emphasize Mendele's ties to Jewish society and his self-proclaimed status as an "everyday" Jew saw one Mendele; those who emphasized the distanced satirist and cynic saw quite another. One critic, borrowing a phrase that Russian critics often apply to Gogol, argued that there really are "two Mendeles," and that this was indicative of Abramovitsh's ambiguous feelings toward traditional Jewish society.[15] Meanwhile, critics who insisted upon keeping Mendele in one piece made various attempts to naturalize his privileged position. Reference was made, for example, to Mendele's travels as a book peddler which, so the argument goes, provide him with a more detached and inclusive perspective than that of those who remain in the towns.[16]

In recent years, on the other hand, attention has shifted from the question of Mendele's identity to that of his function. Emphasizing Mendele's role as intermediary, Dan Miron, for example, argues convincingly that Abramovitsh's use of such a narrative persona (which, as Miron points out, was by no means uncommon in nineteenth-century Yiddish literature) was prompted, on the one hand, by his specific thematic objectives and, on the other, by the special circumstances of the Yiddish writer in the nineteenth century. Thus, well aware of the cultural gap that separated him, a secular, Westernized Jew, from the Jewish masses of the Pale of Settlement whom he wished to address, Abramovitsh created in Mendele a kind of "traveler disguised," a character who spoke the language of the masses and adopted the prose of an "everyday" Jew, yet who could criticize traditional Jewish society from the point of view of a maskil.[17] Similarly focusing upon Mendele's function in the narrative structure, Shalom Luria distinguishes between Mendele's role as "character," "narrator," and "rhetorical figure" in his study of The Beggars' Book. As a rhetorical figure, Luria argues, Mendele constantly evokes visions of Jewish society that contradict or at least provide alternatives to those expressed by Mendele as character or narrator. "If the text presents the words of the ironic narrator," Luria writes, "the figure turns our attention to the non-ironic elements. If the text presents the words of the lyrical-pathetic narrator, we would expect the figure to give expression to the non-pathetic view."[18] The overall effect of this narrative procedure, according to Luria, is the evocation of a complex but "balanced" vision of traditional Jewish society in which contradictions (in point of view, response, evaluation, etc.) are viewed as complementary elements of the total picture.

What Miron's and Luria's studies suggest is that Mendele's "identity," that complex of feelings, thoughts, behavior, and action which we call a character, is in fact dictated, to one degree or another, by his function in the narrative structure. Neither Miron nor Luria, however, pursues the implications of his functional analysis far enough. Both, for example, maintain the notion of "character" and, on occasion, speak of Mendele as if there were indeed some "psychological essence" -- in addition to the functional requisites -- underlying the striking inconsistencies in his behavior. In calling Mendele a traveler disguised, Miron assumes that there must be a "real" Mendele beneath the mask, a "humanist and apostate" who reveals himself only to the reader, and that only sporadically. Luria writes explicitly of Mendele's role "as character," but he never fully explains the function of this aspect of Mendele and, indeed, it is difficult to perceive on what basis he distributes Mendele's words and actions between the three roles he isolates.

Mendele's narrative practice, in fact, prevents us from determining with any degree of confidence just who the "real" Mendele is. Mendele shifts perspectives and attitudes with the ease of a quick-change artist and, what is even more disconcerting, he accomplishes these metamorphoses before our very eyes. At any given moment he can be a naive storyteller or a sophisticated ironist, a pious Jew or an apostate, an "everyday" Jew whose behavior is determined by social and economic circumstances or a detached, cynical observer of that behavior. It is left to the reader to orient himself to these shifts, to fill in the narrative gaps that might explain the inconsistencies. At times, this task may present no great difficulties, and with a little ingenuity the reader will be able to reconstruct a reasonably coherent identity for Mendele. At times, however, even the most ingenious reader, if he is attentive, may have difficulty fitting the pieces together.

Indeed, a careful reading of the first four paragraphs of The Beggars' Book reveals at least four distinct points of view, four potential Mendeles. "When the warm winds blow and sunny days arrive and there is light and joy in the world of the The Holy One Blessed be He," Mendele tells us in the opening lines of his narrative, "days of mourning, fasting, and tears arrive for the Jews one after another..." [H91; Y9]. Only a pious Jew would refer to God as "The Holy One Blessed be He," but Mendele's words clearly subvert traditional piety. With the epigrammatic precision of an accomplished ironist, Mendele articulates the absurd contradiction between the natural order and the Jewish religious calendar that turns the summer months into a period of national mourning. The reference to God in connection with nature, in fact, suggests that mourning during a period of joy in His world goes counter to God's will. And while Mendele is clearly implicated in the Jews' absurd behavior -- he supplies the prayer books and religious paraphernalia which, as he says, are "useful for the spilling of tears" -- he maintains his distance, emphasizing his purely commercial interest in the conduct of his people: "Our people Israel lament and pass the balmy days in tears -- and I turn it to trade." Then, as if he has pushed his irony as far as he dares, Mendele discounts all he has said with his characteristic disclaimer: "... but that's not my point." But of course the point has been made only too well, and Mendele, the master of ironic equivocation, has made sure that his readers know it.

In the next paragraph, however, Mendele adopts the pious stance he has just ridiculed. Wearing <u>tallit</u> and <u>tefillin</u> as required by Jewish law, Mendele recites the morning prayers as he leads his horses absent-mindedly down the road. The beauty of the countryside, "Satan's handiwork," as Mendele now refers to it, tempts him from his religious duties and his thoughts are in conflict. Using traditional rabbinic categories, Mendele tells us how the Good Impulse urges him to close his eyes to nature while the Evil Impulse just as firmly encourages him to look and enjoy to his heart's content. The Evil Impulse apparently gains the upper hand, for Mendele begins to describe "Satan's handiwork" in vivid, sensual detail. This sudden burst of pastoral lyricism throws the neat division between the impulses into disarray and invites the reader to perform an ironic reversal of values. The Evil Impulse no longer appears very sinister and the demands of the Good Impulse remind us of the absurdity laid out for us so clearly in the preceding paragraph. But while the irony is clear, it is no longer obvious who the ironist is. Unlike the self-confident ironist of the first paragraph, this Mendele is taken aback and ashamed of his "evil thoughts" and ultimately rejects the lyricist within him, siding rather with the pietist and the values of the "everyday" Jew. The curses that escape his lips and mingle with his prayers are, for this Mendele, a product of temporary delirium and he feels that he must hide his disgrace from God.

The cover-up is attempted, but in the process a new Mendele suddenly appears. The confusion and inner turmoil vanish and Mendele, now quite deliberately and self-consciously, decides to play the role of an "everyday" Jew. With surprising candor he tells us how he "puts on an innocent expression" and, when that "ruse" does not satisfy him, "puts on a sad face, sighs piously," and returns to his prayers. No longer a pious Jew in conflict with himself, Mendele is now only an impostor whose every move is carefully planned in advance. This, then, is the concealed apostate, the "traveler disguised" pointing to his own mask.

The most dazzling of Mendele's metamorphoses, however, is yet to come. For even though Mendele admits that his recitation of the traditional prayers is only a ruse, it affects him, he tells us, as it would a truly pious Jew. "As soon as a Jew pours out his heart to the Omniscient One and recites a hymn," he notes, "he thinks that he has done all that is in his power and his mind is set at ease, just like a child who, having received his punishment, wipes his tears and is still" [H91; Y8]. Mendele is now the pious Jew he describes and, accordingly, his prayers put his mind at ease. "Lord of the Universe," he proclaims, "I did my part and performed my duty; now it all depends on you" [ibid.].

Mendele's hallucination was not, then, as isolated an incident as it first appeared. It is not only in moments of delirium that Mendele breaks into little pieces; the pieces are, in fact, strewn throughout <u>The Beggars' Book</u>. Mendele's identities can proliferate in this manner because his behavior is not determined by considerations of psychological "realism," because there is no stable center or "psychological essence" underlying and limiting his choice of action. Mendele is simply a voice, or more accurately, a series of voices attached to a proper name that neither add up, reveal psychological depth, nor reward efforts to find human analogies. Thus, questions of psychological motivation, environmental determinants, or moral freedom -- questions that we might legitimately ask of a "character" -- are irrelevant here. Mendele's function, his raison d'être, is to narrate, and in fulfilling this function he must conform to the structural and thematic objectives for which he was created. He simply has no choice in the matter.

While Mendele's multiple narrative identifies clearly subvert the conventions of psychological realism, they serve the needs of the skaz admirably. Through Mendele Abramovitsh can present Jewish society from various angles and diverse postures, exposing its follies from without or subverting its values from within. He can manipulate narrative distance, radically shift point of view, effect sudden modulations of tone and comic juxtapositions, always relying upon Mendele's protean identity, his ability to metamorphose on the spot, to unify the otherwise incompatible stances. Mendele integrates the loose plot (as all first-person narrators tend to do) yet, because he is a series of voices and not a psychological entity, Abramovitsh does not have to face the narrative restrictions imposed by a limited and internally consistent point of view.

Mendele, as we have seen, has a habit of leaping between the extremes of satiric detachment and sentimental identification. In a "character," such violent oscillation might suggest a certain psychological instability, an internal conflict of crucial importance to our understanding of the narrative. In Mendele's case, however, we are not encouraged to probe the psychological depths. On the contrary, whenever Mendele withholds sympathy where it seems called for or deflates his own occasional sentimental outbursts, the reader is encouraged to look outward, to see Jewish society from an unfamiliar perspective and then to re-examine his -- not Mendele's -- response to it. The violent juxtapositions of cynicism and sentimentality are designed to disorient the reader, to jolt him out of accustomed or conventional attitudes toward Jewish society. Just when he least expects it, the reader's emotions are short-circuited and his perceptions subjected to a radical critique. This dislocation of emotions does more than generate ambivalence; it thoroughly undermines the reader's sense of "familiar reality" and forces him to see and respond to Jewish society in unexpected and at times uncomfortable ways.

Mendele's narrative function, then, is nothing less than the methodical defamiliarization of Jewish society. In the guise of a trustworthy guide and intermediary, Mendele subverts and frustrates the reader's expectations every step of the way. Even when Mendele refers to "typical" Jewish practice and behavior he is playing his subversive role, for what he introduces as typical and well-known he invariably describes in a grotesquely exaggerated manner. Thus, rather than contributing to the "reality effect" by grounding the narrative in a familiar social reality (as in conventional nineteenth-century realistic fiction), Mendele's appeals to the "Cultural Code" have a disorienting effect. Once again, the reader is forced to re-examine his habitual perceptions and see Jewish society in a new light. It is not surprising, then, that readers and critics who come to Abramovitsh's works expecting a "realistic" portrait of Jewish life in the Pale, which is to say a reassuring confirmation of their own perceptions and attitudes, are invariably disappointed. Nor is it surprising that some critics have accused Mendele of arrogance, callousness, or some inexplicable deficiency in sympathetic understanding. Such readers, one might argue, are Abramovitsh's chief targets.

Whenever Mendele witholds sympathy, engages in cynical commentary, or debunks conventional sentimentality, he is simply performing the task of defamiliarization for which he was created. Consider, for example, Mendele's apparently callous response to Fishke's tale of innocent suffering. Fishke's tale provides a powerful contrast to Mendele's generally satirical view of Jewish society. Beyond its obviously sentimental and melodramatic elements, one can discern the genuine perplexity of an individual particularly vulnerable to the circumstances of Jewish life in the Pale of Settlement. Fishke is the individual who is concealed in Mendele's categories and generalizations; in telling his story he exposes the pathetic side of Jewish existence that Mendele usually takes great pains to repress. In the light of Fishke's story, Mendele's satire is likely to appear painfully inadequate, his cynicism cruelly frivolous.

How does Mendele respond to the challenge? In the beginning, at least, he seems intent upon helping Fishke tell his story. He encourages Fishke to speak out and spurs him on whenever the going gets tough. And Mendele is obviously concerned that the reader experience the full impact of Fishke's tale. He is, after all, the one who transmits the tale to the reader, and this requires, as Mendele himself points out, translating Fishke's halting and barely coherent Yiddish with the necessary "corrections and clarifications." Mendele serves, then, as Fishke's faithful representative before the reader, providing him with both a voice and a literary medium in which to express his otherwise mute suffering.

At the same time, however, Mendele does his best to subvert the sentimental melodrama that he himself has no small part in creating. As he does with everything else he sees or hears, Mendele uses Fishke's tale as a pretext for comic digression and satiric commentary. Thus, when Fishke attempts to describe the beggars whom he joined while on the road, Mendele seizes the opportunity to indulge in one of his comic anatomies of Jewish society. Listing all the categories and sub-categories of beggars along with details of their characteristic techniques and attitudes, Mendele seems to forget about Fishke and his sad tale altogether. The tide is stemmed only when Reb Alter, always anxious to get to the point, interrupts Mendele and unwittingly supplies the generalization implicit in Mendele's words. "You might as well have cut things short," he complains, "and simply said that every Jew is a beggar" [H115; Y89].

Mendele, however, cannot be stopped for long. Even as Fishke begins to describe his hardships on the road and his wife's cruelty, Mendele's mind is still occupied with his lists and categories. When Fishke relates a particularly unpleasant episode with his wife, Mendele cries out in glee that he has just thought of another category. Cutting Fishke short, he describes the practice of a certain beggar in Kisalon who considered the town a kind of personal fiefdom and went so far as to maintain records of all the householders who "owed" him handouts. As Fishke continues, the gap between his pathetic tale and Mendele's response grows wider. Fishke tells how his wife bullied him into accepting a rather ominous invitation to join a band of beggars, adding that "only God in heaven knew the depth of my misery at that moment" [H117; Y97]. Ignoring Fishke's pathetic outburst, Mendele is merely reminded of his relative Haya-Traina and her hen-picked husband. "It appears to me," he comments light-heartedly, "that our Fishke, too, receives sure blows from his wife from time to time" [H117; Y97].

Even while Mendele admits that there is a certain naive eloquence to Fishke's tale, he cannot resist the temptation of poking fun at Fishke's sudden inspiration. Like Balaam's ass, boring preachers, and "the worst of cantors," Mendele explains, Fishke, too, has his moment of glory, surprising us with unaccustomed eloquence before lapsing into his usual boorishness. Fishke, Mendele tells us, is like a golem requiring special care. To be sure, Mendele admits, animating this particular golem does not require any esoteric knowledge, but, then again, "all ages are not equal, and neither are their golems" [H123; Y120].[19]

Mendele seems, then, particularly two-faced in his response to Fishke's tale. From one side he retells the tale, improving it with the necessary corrections and clarifications in order to make sure that the reader experiences the full impact of Fishke's plight. At the same time, he himself ignores that plight and subverts the pathetic melodrama with satiric digressions, ironic commentaries, and cynical asides. Once again, Mendele presents us with a seemingly irresolvable psychological puzzle. Is he really of two minds about Fishke's plight? Is he, for some reason unknown to us, attempting to cover up his real feelings? And if so, from whom? Does his inconsistency indicate some deep-rooted inner conflict? These questions are resolved -- are in fact rendered irrelevant -- once we realize that Mendele is not a "character" whose behavior must form a more or less coherent pattern based upon our notions of psychological realism. His narrative activity is not designed to reveal psychological complication nor does it provide any basis for a reconstruction of a coherent, meaningful identity. As a narrative device, Mendele's function is to transform potentially pathetic situations into comic narrative, to evoke and deflate conventional sentimentality, in sum, to prevent the reader from adopting a monocular view of Jewish society. In order to effect the disorienting juxtapositions required for this task, Abramovitsh is prepared to stretch and finally shatter Mendele's "psychological essence." Psychological realism is subjugated -- and subverted -- by the requirements of the narrative.

Abramovitsh, to be sure, does not ignore altogether the demands of conventional realistic characterization. Unlike the "self-conscious" novelists of the eighteenth and twentieth centuries, he is not intent upon laying bare his technique in order to flaunt the narrative artifice. His concerns are sociological, not epistemological, and thus, like most nineteenth-century "readerly" novelists, he attempts to conceal technique and convention, to pass them off as unmediated or "innocent" (i.e., "realistic") representations of reality.[20] Significantly, however, Abramovitsh's most direct attempt to anchor Mendele's narrative activity in a specific identity with a unique personal history appears outside of the narrative structures in which he appears. This attempt at naturalizing Mendele takes the form of a biographical sketch which has been included in a number of editions of Abramovitsh's collected works.[21] In the sketch, Mendele offers a few scattered details about his childhood and early years, mentions his wife and children, and describes his own physical appearance. Then, after reluctantly revealing these details for his "prying readers," he suggests that those who desire more specific information address him privately. Even the few details that are provided, however, go far beyond anything we get in the works themselves. Such details are absent from the works because, as Mendele's reluctance here suggests, they are irrelevant. They would serve no function and, indeed, they might undermine Abramovitsh's thematic objectives by invalidating the process of defamiliarization, reducing it to the product of a subjective and therefore unreliable point of view.

Mendele is a character in pieces or, rather, not a character at all but a collection of identities, a "figure," in the Structuralist vernacular, that cannot be analyzed in terms of "biography, psychology, or time."[22] Still, we must account for the fact that more than four generations of readers and critics have perceived him as a character and, indeed, one of the most vivid and engaging characters in all of Hebrew fiction. Should we dismiss this perception as simply a naive response to the literary text or, worse, as interpretive tendentiousness? The impulse to find human analogies for fictional characters is surely not, as some Structuralist theories seem to suggest, an "incorrect" one. It is firmly rooted in the mimetic tradition of fiction; indeed, every fictional character and every plot would be incomprehensible were we forbidden -- as if that were possible -- to draw upon our knowledge of human experience in order to "name" them.[23] But how can we explain the fact that Mendele, for whom the human analogy breaks down as soon as we pursue it with any consistency, continues to fascinate us?

The answer lies in the very fact that Mendele does not cohere as a character, that we cannot understand and categorize him as we can, for example, static characters like Reb Alter and Fishke. When a narrative personage acts strangely or deviates from human experience as we understand it, our first response is to naturalize the apparent deviation. Otherwise, we would be forced to conclude that the character is simply "unrealistic" and that, if it is realism we are looking for, we are wasting our time. Thus, paradoxically, the less sense a character makes, the more interesting and psychologically complex he is likely to appear. Mendele's interest as a character and the fascination he exerts, then, are by-products of his narrative function which, as we have seen, forces him to act "strangely." Because we can never identify Mendele with complete confidence, because all attempts at psychological reconstruction are bound to end in irresolvable contradiction, Mendele seems to conceal depths that continually invite new soundings.

This illusion of depth -- for it is an illusion -- is what sets Mendele apart from the other characters that populate Abramovitsh's fictional world. Characters like Reb Alter and Fishke make complete sense. They act and think with complete consistency because they are imprisoned by their environment and because Mendele presents them to us as stereotypes. Thoroughly conditioned to respond according to socially determined patterns, they can be pathetic or comic victims of circumstance, but never anything more. Because Mendele refuses to make sense, because his behavior is always unpredictable and often contradictory, he seems to transcend the social and economic circumstances in which the others are trapped. Mendele's narrative multiplicity is a form of liberation, a claim to autonomy in the face of overwhelming circumstances. Like a tightrope walker who constantly shifts his weight in order to defy the force of gravity, Mendele seems to confront and struggle with his environment, constantly shifting his ground to avoid entrapment. Precisely because he cannot be pinned down or categorized, Mendele seems to project a sense of self in a world of social stereotypes. Ironically, the very effort to provide a definitive reconstruction of Mendele's "identity" -- to fit the pieces together -- denies this sense of autonomy.

CHAPTER FOUR

The Drama of Narration: Y.H. Brenner's In Winter

And in truth, what can I tell of our life in my generation? Great and mysterious deeds! Not I nor the house of my father have thrilled the world with our deeds. Dukes, governors, generals, and warriors we have not been; after beautiful women and pretty maidens we have not lusted; to clash like rams one man against another or to stand witness to the duel we have not attempted; how to dance with young wives and maidens at the wine feast we know not; to hunt the live prey over field and forest we have not set out; to the ends of the earth or distant seas we have not travelled nor have we discovered any new continents; we have not indulged in games of chance nor wasted our money on princes and princesses or the pleasures of the flesh. In short, all the tid-bits that make for a pleasant and entertaining tale are not to be found among us. Instead, we have the school room and country tutor, match-makers, impoverished families, deserted wives, widows and orphans, the homeless and the bankrupt, sabbath and holiday beggars, indigents, alms collectors, and charity officials, all kinds of calamities, all kinds of poverty, want, and destitution, all kinds of queer ways of making a living. This is our life, God help us! A gloomy existence with no satisfaction or peace, no glory, grandeur, or brilliance; a life that is like a stale morsel of food, lacking all flavor and delight.

I have made myself a notebook of blank paper, and I intend to write some notes and sketches from "my life" --

"My life" -- in quotation marks: For I have no future or present; only the past remains --

The past! ...If someone were to hear my last remark he would think, certainly, that I had some awe-inspiring events to recount from "my past," some appalling, frightening, heart-rending tragedy --

But such is hardly the case! For in my past there are no intriguing plots, no sentimental moments, no terrible tragedies; neither are there murders, love affairs nor even games of chance and sudden inheritances; there are only shadow-like men, dim visions, hidden tears, sighs...

My past is not the past of a hero because, quite simply, I myself am not a hero.

I am a young tutor in this village.

But in spite of this, in spite of that fact that I am not a hero, I want to record my past, my non-heroic past. The tales of heroes are written to thrill the public. My past, the past of an anti-hero, I write for myself and in secret.

And even this introduction is superfluous.

These two passages, the first from S.Y. Abramovitsh's In Those Days[1] and the second from Y.H. Brenner's In Winter,[2] show some striking similarities. Both are the statements of narrator-heroes who will shortly tell the stories of their lives. Both speakers complain of the difficulties they must overcome in pursuing this task, and, for both, those difficulties involve what their stories must, of necessity, lack. Their stories, both insist, can have little in common with romantic tales of conflict and violence, love and lust, adventure and discovery. "All the tid-bits that make for a pleasant and entertaining tale," Reb Shelomo complains, "are not to be found among us." Seeming to echo Reb Shelomo's words, Brenner's Feuermann speaks of the absence of "intriguing plots, sentimental moments, and terrible tragedies" in his past. Both stress that their stories can have no heroes, or at least not the type of hero that readers of romantic tales have come to expect. Reb Shelomo complains that his world contains no "dukes, governors, generals, and warriors." "I myself am not a hero," laments Feuermann.

Moreover, the first-person autobiographical mode in which both passages are written encourages us, in each case, to consider the identity of the speaker. For as soon as the speaker makes his presence explicit with the pronoun "I" (and in each passage he does so in the very first line), the reader is forced to consider a matter which, in third-person narratives, is generally forgotten, or, by convention, considered irrelevant, namely, what Gérard Genette calls the "narrating instance."[3] Who is this "I" and why is he writing this story? Where and under what circumstances did he write it? How much time has elapsed since the events he is recounting took place? Now while first-person narrative may provoke these questions, it does not have to provide answers for them. It may, in fact, ignore them in part or whole. This is, as we have argued, precisely the case in Abramovitsh's The Beggars' Book. The utterances of the narrator-hero of that novel, Mendele Mokher Sefarim, are not dictated by his "character," but rather by the thematic preoccupations of his creator. The circumstances in which he writes his tale are never alluded to. Indeed, while Mendele clearly recounts his adventures on the road to Kisalon at some point after they have taken place, it often appears as if the action and writing take place simultaneously. Mendele's "character" ultimately breaks into pieces and we are confronted with a series of voices that do not coalesce into a coherent psychological structure.

The "character" of Reb Shelomo, of course, does not break apart in this manner, at least not in the passage we have quoted. Still, like Mendele, Reb Shelomo directs our attention outward, toward the world that surrounds him rather to himself. Thus, even though he begins by addressing his own problems as a writer and artist, his focus quickly shifts from his individual fate to that of Jewish society as a whole. By the fourth sentence, the first-person singular has given way to the first-person plural: it is what "we" are not, what "we" lack, what "our" life is like that concern Reb Shelomo. Thus, his statement evolves into an overview of traditional Jewish society, one of those sweeping anatomies in which Mendele so often indulges. "This is our life," Reb Shelomo concludes, "a gloomy existence, with no satisfaction or peace, no glory, grandeur or brilliance." The logic of the first-person narrative is not subverted, but it is also not pursued. The autobiographical narrative that this passage introduces is written in the third person.

In In Winter, on the other hand, the narrating instance is clearly and insistently foregrounded. Every utterance of the narrating "I" provides us with access to his personality, serves as an expression or symptom of his "character." This is, of course, Todorov's definition, slightly wrenched from context, of psychological fiction, and it is not too difficult to analyze the passage we have quoted in terms of the psychology of the speaker, Yermiah Feuermann. Feuermann is obviously obsessed with feelings of inferiority, of his lack, as he sees it, of a real past, and his failure to attain some heroic ideal. Moreover, an exaggerated, almost morbid self-consciousness prevents him from writing with confidence about himself or his motives, including the motives that lead him to write the story of his life. The very notion of "my life" must, for Feuermann, be surrounded by quotation marks, hemmed in with reservations, explanations, objections. The very possibility of telling one's story, even in the form of "notes and sketches," is, from the beginning, cast into doubt. The whole enterprise, finally, loses all relation to the public and becomes instead a kind of confession to be carried out for oneself "in secret."

Far from an anatomy of traditional Jewish society, then, Feuermann's statement is the tormented confession of an individual whose gaze is fixed inward. Compared to Reb Shelomo's expansive vision, Feuermann's point of view is utterly claustrophobic. What little is reflected of Jewish society comes in the form of fragments of memory, vague feelings, floating anxieties. In place of Reb Shelomo's sharply delineated social types, Feuermann evokes a nightmare world populated by shadow-like men and disembodied sighs.

In spite of the similarities between the two passages, then, the differences between them are substantial and, indeed, signal a major development in modern Hebrew fiction, a shift in focus from the group to the individual, from a concern with broad social and national issues to the "individualization" of character and the exploration of the inner workings of the human psyche.[4] Micah Yosef Berdyczweski, whose works had a profound influence on Brenner, was among the first to perceive the special quality of the younger writer's fiction. Responding to Brenner's first collection of short stories, Berdyczweski marveled that his characters had only to speak and they "stand before us naked, revealing all that is within."[5] And even Bialik, who was troubled by Brenner's fiction on other grounds, had to admit his impatience with literary theories when, as he put it, he was able to see "a living soul."[6]

Much of the early reaction to Brenner, however, was not so positive. Critics who were under the spell of Ahad Ha-Am's positivism accused Brenner of abandoning the social mission of modern Hebrew literature. By dwelling upon the inner life of a few egocentric individuals cut off from the rest of society, Brenner, they argued, could hardly contribute to the national struggle. Moreover, by choosing such "negative" types as his protagonists, he was actually doing a disservice to the struggle for national revival. Y.A.

Lubitzki, reacting to Brenner's protagonists as though they represented a personal affront, dismissed them as "miserable adolescents and loafers."[7] Later, Shelomo Tsemah was to accuse Brenner of a "lack of imagination and an inability to see anything but the ugly." Brenner's characters, Tsemah complained, were fashioned from "worn out rotten material" and even then Brenner could only see the "evil that is within them."[8]

The critics who came to Brenner's defense met his accusors on their own ground. Writing enthusiastically of In Winter in the Russian Jewish press, H.Y. Katzenelson argued that Brenner's progatonists, far from being mere malcontents or the projections of a sick mind, were the "genuine representatives of the new generation." Borrowing his terms from contemporary Russian literary criticism, Katzenelson described the collective fate of these individuals in language that, in Hebrew translation, was to become standard in defining this new "national type." Having broken their ties with traditional Jewish society, he wrote, Brenner's protagonists had become "superfluous, broken men, uprooted from one world yet not having arrived in another."[9] For Ba'al Mahshavot, another of Brenner's early admirers, the two main protagonists in Brenner's second novel, Beside the Point, were "symbols of the fragmented, wretched souls that fill the new generation." They are, he wrote, "the victims of an age of transition."[10]

In their attempt to domesticate Brenner's protagonists, then, the younger critics argued that the talush, or uprooted man, of Brenner's fiction was no less typical than Abramovitsh's national types, no less the product -- indeed the victim -- of his environment. The environment, they argued, had changed radically since the time of Abramovitsh's "everyday Jews," and so had the national type. The private torments and obsessions of the talush, his very fate, reflected a society caught in the grips of social upheaval and radical transformation. If, in his struggle between the burdens of the past and the imperatives of the present, the talush often falls victim to madness or suicide, this is only because the nation itself was suffering from extreme spiritual malaise. The talush, Shimon Halkin would later say, is a "sign for the generations" of the "general uprooting" that had taken place in Jewish life in the modern world.[11]

This socially oriented approach toward Brenner's protagonists dominated Hebrew criticism through the 1950's and went hand in hand with a growing tendency on the part of the critics and the public alike to see in these fictional personages direct autobiographical representations of the author himself. As a result, Brenner's novels were often treated as sociological documents, first-hand accounts of the ills afflicting the nation as a whole. The very term talush slipped into common usage and was soon used indiscriminately to describe any number of literary and extra-literary personages suffering the pangs of modernity. Not only Brenner's protagonists, but those of Feierberg, Bershadski, Berdyczewski, Gnessin, Shofman, Berkovitz, and others were all described as t'lushim, all examples of the new national type.

Now there clearly is a relationship between the shifting circumstances of Jewish life in Eastern Europe at the turn of the century and the kind of protagonist the younger novelists of that period were producing. A figure like the talush, as he appears in Brenner's novels, was unlikely to appear, for example, in the literature of the early

Haskalah. A sizeable and restless Intelligentsia estranged from traditional Jewish society yet disillusioned by Western culture did not yet exist, and the maskilim themselves did not foresee the true dimensions of the coming conflict. Braced by their nineteenth-century optimism, they looked forward to a successful synthesis of tradition and modernity, once, that is, the Jews could be convinced to abandon the vestiges of medievalism in their midst. Even Abramovitsh, who no longer shared the optimism of the early maskilim, continued to direct his satire at traditional Jewish society. The rising currents of change both within and outside of Jewish society only occasionally ripple the surface of the static world he portrays, and the disillusioned intelligentsia barely finds a place in his gallery of national types. In turning to this group for their protagonists, often in a deeply autobiographical way, the younger writers, as F. Lahover was quick to perceive, affected a major shift in the direction of Hebrew fiction, establishing the unfolding, dynamic present as the proper sphere of the novelist, rather than the near or distant past.[12]

Analyzing literary characters, however, in terms of a social context that lies beyond the novel has its dangers. Complex characters tend to be flattened out in order to fit preconceived sociological or historical schemata. Detail and nuance are often sacrificed for the sake of generalization, specificity is lost in the effort to establish workable categories. Thus, the term talush has been applied to so many protagonists of so many Hebrew novels that its original explanatory power has been considerably diminished. Further, one is tempted to analyze the environment in terms of one overall conception, making it possible to "explain" everything in one neat formulation. Baruch Kurzweil, for example, argues that the exclusive origin of the problems of Brenner's t'lushim, including their sexual difficulties, is the breakdown of religion and the loss of God. For Kurzweil, there is no such thing as a private tragedy in Brenner's works; there is only a national tragedy. The protagonist's "private eternal Winter is the symptom of the winter of the nation."[13]

But most importantly, this approach ignores the very thing that sets Brenner's fiction off from that of the earlier Hebrew novelists, and that, moreover, places it squarely in the tradition of modern psychological fiction. For in Brenner's fiction we are not simply faced with a shift in focus from the group to the individual but with an epistemological revolution, a radical redefinition of the "truth" that fiction purports to tell. As in the works of Joyce, Woolf, and Proust, the fictional world in Brenner's novels is not presented as an independent and objective reality in which various characters, of varying degrees of individuality, pursue their fates. Rather, the fictional world is typically revealed to the reader as it impinges upon the consciousness of the character; what we "see" is the imprint of experience upon consciousness, seldom experience itself. Thus, the true object of representation in the modern psychological novel is, to use Leon Edel's phrase (borrowed from Henry James), the "atmosphere of the mind," the act of perception itself and the manner in which it is complicated by the processes of the mind.[14] Brenner described much the same thing when he wrote, in response to criticism of his novel, From Here and There, that it was not his intention to show "how things appear to an objective, clear-headed observer," but rather to evoke an "atmosphere" as it is perceived by a particular individual.[15] In Brenner's novels, and in the modern psychological novel in general, the consciousness of the protagonist is the medium, as it were, in which all else is suspended and, as such, it constitutes the center of narrative interest.

* * *

In Winter is the fictional autobiography of Yermiah Feuermann, a young Jewish intellectual in Russia at the turn of the last century. Raised and educated according to the established modes of traditional Jewish society, he suffers a religious crisis at an early age and, having lost his faith, attempts to find a place for himself among the conflicting value systems and ideologies of the modern world. He is hampered in these efforts, however, by his inability to break his psychological ties to his past, particularly to his father who is an object of both hatred and guilt, and by his own deep-seated feelings of inferiority that burst out, at times, in bitter expressions of self-hatred. Feuermann, then, is caught between two worlds, neither of which can offer him a home. This situation, reflected externally in his restless travels between his home town and the city N., leads eventually to psychological and spiritual paralysis, an internal season of "Winter."

Neither the autobiographical form of In Winter nor the first-person mode in which it is narrated, however, make Brenner's novella an example of modern psychological fiction as I have attempted to define it. Indeed, modern psychological novelists have generally preferred omniscient third-person narrators in order to avoid the restrictions imposed by a fixed and limited point of view as well as the loss of immediacy in the presentation of the "atmosphere of the mind" that results from the inevitably retrospective nature of first-person narrative.[16] Brenner himself employed third-person narrative in other works, and we shall analyze how he manipulates that mode of narration for the purposes of psychological fiction in his last novel, Breakdown and Bereavement, in Chapter V. What makes the first-person autobiographical narrative of In Winter an example of modern psychological fiction is the manner and degree to which Brenner exploits the logic of the first-person narrative by foregrounding the narrating instance. Indeed, we may propose the general rule that first-person narrative is "psychological" to the degree that a knowledge of the narrating instance is necessary to our understanding of the text, to the degree, in other works, that it serves as the regulating principle of the narrative structure. As we shall see, in In Winter, the narrating instance is indeed the regulating principle. The choice of events that are narrated, the manner in which they are narrated, and the ways in which they are linked to each other and integrated into the overall structure are not dictated by some intrinsic logic of events but rather by the narrator's relation to those events as mediated through his memory.

Gershon Shaked and Yosef Ewen, two critics who have made important contributions to the analysis of Brenner's narrative art, have recognized the importance of the narrating instance in In Winter.[17] Drawing upon Bertril Romberg's study of first-person narrative,[18] they emphasize two aspects of its "logic" that are crucial to any analysis of the novella. In drawing attention to the narrating instance, first-person narrative also draws attention to the temporal distance between the events that are described in the narrative and the act of narrating itself. Thus, one must distinguish between the "narrated time" and the "time of narration" and take this distinction into consideration when analyzing the narrator's attitude toward the events he narrates as well as the manner in which he narrates them. In autobiographical first-person narrative, this distinction is particularly crucial, for temporal distance almost inevitably leads to psychological distance. Thus, the classic confrontation in autobiographical narrative is between the mature, knowledgeable, and dispassionate "narrating I" and the more naive and foolish "experiencing I."[19] Applying these distinctions to In Winter, Shaked and Ewen trace the variety of attitudes that Yermiah Feuermann, as narrating I, displays toward his earlier avatar, the experiencing I. For Shaked, that attitude is essentially ironic and judgmental -- the narrating I brings the experiencing I before the "throne of judgment" -- although he notes a relaxing of the irony toward the end of the narrative. In Ewen's analysis, Feuermann's attitude swings between the poles of total identification with his earlier self (the "near view") and total ironic rejection (the "distant view"). In both analyses, the emphasis falls upon Feuermann's ability to distance himself from his past and regard his earlier selves with the liberating irony that is only available to an "older but wiser" narrating I.

In Winter, however, does not entirely conform to Romberg's schema, and it is, I would suggest, precisely the novella's deviations from classic autobiographical narrative that account for much of its power. Feuermann clearly lacks the intellectual and emotional distance from his past which, in classic autobiographical narrative, enables the retrospective narrator to structure his past into a meaningful and coherent whole and to maintain a consistently ironic stance toward his earlier selves. On the contrary, the past for Feuermann is still laden with highly charged emotions, still, as he sits down to write his "notes and sketches," a painful and rather mysterious burden. The very relationship between his past and present circumstances -- whether he is a product of his "wretched" past or his past is simply a reflection of his own innate deficiencies -- is a matter of some confusion to Feuermann:

> Yes, my past is gloomy, wretched, and vulgar because it is mine, the past of a man like me; and yet, to a great degree, I am what I am because I have a past like that, a past of littleness, a gloomy, wretched, and vulgar past.[20]

Rather than a retrospective summing up, Feuermann's narrative enterprise is an act of introspection, an obsessive exercise in self-analysis and accusation. The model that Genette proposes for this type of "testimonial" narrative is Rousseau's Confessions: "In writing this," Rouseau states at one point, "I feel my pulse quicken yet."[21] It is this quickening of the pulse that takes place in the narrating instance that forms the central drama of In Winter, a drama composed not of narrated events but of the act of narration itself.

The nature of this drama is laid out for us in the first paragraphs of the novella. Feuermann not only announces his intention to write some "notes and sketches" on his life, he expresses in no uncertain terms his attitude both toward his past and his efforts to write about it. "My past," Feuermann asserts, "is not the past of a hero because, quite simply, I myself am not a hero" (7). Feuermann is both repelled and fascinated by his past, or, as he sees it, his lack of a "heroic" past. He cannot free himself from that past, nor from the need he feels to write about it, but at the same time he must drain it of all significance, find in it only further justification for his cynicism and self-hatred. Thus, each time he asserts the possibility of narrating his past, even in the form of "notes and sketches," he immediately, impulsively retracts the assertion and retreats into an attitude of disillusionment and self-denigration. Still, even though he knows that his story has no hope of "thrilling" the public, he must write it. "My past," he concludes, "the past of a non-hero, I write for myself and in secret" (7).

This syndrome of attraction and repulsion which, as Dan Miron has pointed out, is reflected in the very syntax of this opening statement,[22] forms the basis of the drama of narration that follows. Feuermann will indeed evoke moments and scenes from his past, but they will not form a coherent or complete autobiographical narrative. Rather, they will remain isolated and fragmentary memories rocked by varying degrees and combinations of attraction and repulsion. At times the narrative is full of empathy and pity toward the child who is victimized and persecuted by his father, his schoolmates in the heder, later by the head of the yeshiva, and still later by the gentiles and assimilated Jews of the city N. where he attempts to learn of the world beyond the confines of Jewish tradition. At other times, Feuermann's narrative seethes with self-hatred and loathing toward what he considers his weakness and inadequacies, his inability to gain the knowledge of the world he so desires, his obsessions with self-analysis and doubt, and especially his ambivalent and confused feelings toward women.

When Feuermann sits down to write his notes and sketches, few if any of the conflicts that plagued him in the past have been resolved. Thus, far from the object of retrospective evocation and analysis, these conflicts are very much a part of the narrating instance. At one point, Feuermann denies the very notion of a past that exists beyond the present moment of recollection:

> The shape of my past is completely hidden from the eye of my memory [...] and the isolated facts that have escaped the upheaval, of which I know more than I remember [...] do not combine into flesh and blood to form a whole body [...] (9-10)

Feuermann "knows" rather than "remembers" the isolated facts of his past: chronologically of the past, psychologically they belong to the present. As a result, Feuermann cannot distance himself from the events and inner conflicts that form the object of his narrative, cannot consistently maintain the perspective of an "older but wiser" autobiographer who can separate himself from his past selves through a liberating irony.

The manner in which the narrating instance (and the unresolved conflicts it contains) impinge upon the narrative of past events can be seen most clearly in Feuermann's efforts to describe his relations with women. In the course of his narrative Feuermann returns to this subject repeatedly, and every time he does the traces of the narrating instance are unmistakable. The very first time the subject comes up we see with what difficulty and hesitation he approaches the still sensitive issue. Feuermann is recalling his studies at the home of Reb Hanan-Natan and the three daughters of the rabbi's boarder who occupied the thoughts of the older students "more than Reb Hanan-Natan's <u>Seder Nashim</u>."

> [...] and in Obadiah's heart, the son of the rabbi himself, there was "sympathy" -- I have already forgotten toward whom... it seems to me... no, also toward the youngest one. She was a full bodied girl, with cherry lips, a high bosom, and a mouth that was always ringing with laughter. But that's not relevant here. What I meant to do was only to note that I, who was quite distanced from these matters, was ashamed of them from the bottom of my heart. (14)
>
> (Unbracketed ellipses are Brenner's.)

Feuermann's forgetting and then remembering which of the three sisters was the object of Obadiah's "sympathy," is, of course, an action that takes place in the narrating instance. It is as if we are reading an unedited first draft in which we can see not only the results of Feuermann's struggle to tell his story, but the struggle itself. Even after the initial effort to remember meets with success, moreover, the struggle continues. For Feuermann's vivid memories of the youngest daughter, memories that focus upon her sensuality and vitality, catch him by surprise, as it were, and he feels called upon not only to interrupt and dismiss the description ("But that's not relevant here."), but to attempt to explain and even justify this "digression" from his real narrative intentions. Feuermann's claim that he was in fact "quite distanced from these matters," however, is hardly convincing. The struggle reflected in this first attempt to raise the issue of Eros in his narrative offers far more convincing evidence to the contrary.

In the pages that follow Feuermann expends a great deal of energy and words trying to explain the sources of his confused and contradictory feelings toward women. The distance and shame he feels in their presence are, he admits, "the extreme opposite of coldness and purity." In fact, he is obsessed and tormented by his desires, on the one hand, and his feelings of inadequacy and guilt, on the other. Ugly, clumsy, and uncouth by his own estimation, he is sure that he is simply a "burden to the daughters of Eve," an object of scorn and laughter. Yet his feelings of physical inadequacy in no way diminish his desires which, in his eyes, are made no less sinful by the fact that he cannot fulfill them. "How shall I lift my head before my Creator? Is this fitting for a fighter of the <u>kelipot</u>?" Even after he leaves the world of the <u>bet midrash</u> for "the air of the world," desire and guilt still dominate his relations with women. Either they are the object of his all-consuming need to love and be loved, "even if I will only suffer from such a love," or they are useless creatures that are unworthy of him.

> In such a state of mind I knew several young women: Nerman, Lerner, and her... Rachel Mohisevnah... But enough. Here art is needed -- something which the last pages testify I have little of. I have filled a page with words and words -- and I have said nothing. Indeed, my very effort to explain everything is stupid. As much as I add nuance to nuance -- still, that essential, secret hidden thing will remain locked deep inside of me. (15-16)

After having filled a page (in fact many pages) with "words and words," Feuermann comes to the conclusion that, in fact, he has explained nothing. At first, he attributes this to his <u>artistic</u> limitations, as if the difficulty is simply a matter of finding the proper mode of expression. But he immediately realizes that the very effort to "explain everything" is doomed to failure. The hidden essence which he is struggling to express remains hidden precisely because it is still "deep inside," still a controlling obsession of his present struggle.

It must remain hidden and unexplained (although Feuermann will fill more pages with "words and words" on the subject) also because the very words that Feuermann must use are bound to give a false prestige to what, in his view, are feelings deserving only scorn. Here is Feuermann, seven chapters later, still struggling to sort out his feelings toward Rachel Mohisevnah:

> And my feelings of attraction to that same young woman... No, no! What love? Why do people use that noble and precious word at all for that feeling which a <u>man</u> feels for some young woman, even if that feeling of attraction is powerful, creative, complex, and not simply naked, overpowering lust? And thus... but no... I return to the subject of Haimovitz. (30)

Having rejected but not entirely freed himself from his religiously inspired guilt toward sex, Feuermann cannot allow himself to use the "noble and precious word" to describe what he can only view as his lust. Indeed, the residue of his religious struggles is so powerful that even the attraction of a "normal" man toward a woman does not deserve the name love. Thus, even before writing the word, in the space of time that it takes to put pen to paper, as it were, Feuermann recoils from his original impulse to use it. What we read, which takes the form of a complaint about the haphazard way in which people use the word, is the outcome of a struggle taking place in the narrating instance. Feuermann's attempt to evoke a struggle that took place in the "narrated time" only serves to produce one in the "time of narration."

Feuermann describes his erotic conflicts with difficulty and hesitation, with self-denigration and condemnation, because the issue is still sensitive, the crisis still unresolved. It is, quite simply, extremely painful for him to recall events and feelings from which he has not yet recovered, far more painful, he insists, than "picking in a wound" (41). The pain is so great, in fact, that Feuermann must defend himself by denying any autobiographical significance to his frustrated longings, even as he returns to them again and again.

> Here was, it is true, a common occurrence, but a passing one that does not add anything to an understanding of my essential being, a meaningless occurrence. (41)

Just as the life that Feuermann sets out to narrate is only a life in quotation marks which, nevertheless, he feels he must record, so his erotic conflicts, which play such a central role in that life, are finally dismissed as meaningless.

Feuermann's obsessive efforts to analyze his erotic difficulties, of course, belie this particular retraction. His feelings of shame and sexual inadequacy are clearly central elements of his present attitude toward himself and, as such, are a major factor in his inability to write of his past from the comfortable distance of retrospective irony. Indeed, when Feuermann attempts to narrate his encounters with women, the temporal distance between event and narration of event tends to collapse, creating a temporal ambiguity indicative of the unresolved state of the conflict. Consider, for example, the following passage in which Feuermann recalls his feelings after his first encounter with Rachel Mohisevnah in the presence of Borsif, whom he considers his sexual rival:

> When I left, there was only deep hatred in my heart toward Borsif, hatred toward his forelock, his laughter, his vest, the buttons on his coat -- a hatred the like of which I had never known to that day. Clearly, that hatred was caused by my envy, envy toward the free and sublime gestures of that man... by way of comparison, I recalled my own unbecoming, unnatural laughter, my slow negligent gestures, my stuttering words -- and it all seemed so loathsome to me, so stupid and base... and she noticed it -- of course she noticed... Who? A provincial heroine? -- No, I am truly stupid and base! Why do I use such a "banal" term? What wrong did I find in her? A girl like all the girls! And yet... what is there between us anyway? (41-2)

As is characteristic of Brenner's prose, the narration of a past event slides into what Dorrit Cohn calls "self-narrated monologue," the equivalent of "narrated monologue" or le style indirect libre in third-person narrative.[23] When evoking thoughts or feelings of an earlier time, Feuermann renders the movements of his mind as if they were happening in the present, rather than offering a retrospective summary or analysis. In general, these passages are more or less clearly framed by obviously retrospective passages, and thus the reader has little difficulty in transforming the grammatical present tense into the narrative past tense. What is especially interesting about this passage, however, is what happens within the self-narrated monologue itself in regard to time.

The passage begins, conventionally enough, with a past tense and clearly retrospective notation of the moment in question. From this retrospective vantage, Feuermann can point out both the unprecedented intensity of his hatred and its source. When Feuermann begins to evoke his unspoken thoughts in self-narrated monologue, however, we are faced with some difficulties. The past tense verb that introduces the monologue ("I remembered...") is followed by two verbs ("It all seemed... she noticed...") whose temporal status is ambiguous. Does the verb "it seemed," express the narrating I's recollection of his earlier feelings or the experiencing I's recollection of his feelings while in the presence of Rachel and Borsif? Is the conclusion that "she noticed" drawn by Feuermann only now, as he recalls and narrates the past event, or was it drawn by Feuermann at the time of which he writes? The present tense verbs that follow ("I am... stupid... Why do I use...?") only add to the confusion. Is Feuermann quoting, as it were, the thoughts that ran through his mind at that particular moment out of the past, or is he calling himself stupid and questioning his use of a "banal" term now, in the narrating instance, and thus making a statement about his narrative? What, finally, are we to make of the juxtaposition of tenses at the end of the passage ("What did I find in her... what is there between us anyway?")? Are we dealing here with past or present emotions? Is the very style of the passage, with its fragmented syntax, its ellipses, dashes, question marks, and exclamation points, a rendering of earlier emotional conflicts, or an indication of difficulties in the narrating instance?

The temporal confusion of the passage, whether it is a result of conscious artistic choice or simply intuition, is certainly no flaw. It is, in fact, what gives the passage its particular power and intensity. Temporal distinctions collapse, past and present overlap, merge, and finally become indistinguishable because the erotic conflict at the heart of the matter has not been resolved. Feuermann cannot evoke this moment from his past from a comfortable retrospective distance because it is not simply a memory but, as he would put it, a "fact" of the present from which he can never escape.

Feuermann cannot relegate his memories to the comfortable otherness of the past. But why does he feel compelled to commit those memories to writing? What is the source of the obsession that forces him to record a past that can only cause him pain and from which, in any case, he denies all significance? Toward the end of the narrative, Feuermann attempts to answer these questions: "I write," he says, "only because it is impossible for me not to cry out in despair, because I shall never stop lamenting the old pain... yes, never... until my last moment..." (57). But what is to be gained from such a cry of despair? The condensed symbolism of a recurring nightmare that plagues Feuermann during his final stay in his home town, a nightmare in which "childhood dreams were intermingled with my latest impressions," provides some clues:

> I am in a filthy sack. A pile of sand covers my head and heavy stones hold down my hands and legs. I burst out of the sack -- my father strikes me from above. I am a fly playing upon the cheek of that same young woman... She grabs my wings and tears them off... The pain is similar to that which I used to feel in my childhood, when I would see Hell in my dreams... seven circles of ice... step after step... I am climbing... descending... everyone laments for me. (56)

Feuermann's childhood, with its emotional burden of helplessness and claustrophobic entrapment, is evoked in the image of the filthy sack, while the father who, as Dov Sadan has pointed out, constitutes one of the central obsessions of all of Brenner's protagonists, appears as the child's implacable foe.[24] If that sack represents the womb, then the father is not only threatening the child's life, he is attempting to prevent his very birth. The fear of the father is juxtaposed in the dream with another, not unrelated fear, that provoked by the erotic woman. Feuermann sees himself as a repugnant insect whose wings the young woman casually rips off, a symbolic act of castration. In both cases, Feuermann sees himself as a victim, but as the imagery of the dream suggests ("a dirty sack," "a fly") Feuermann also sees himself as a repulsive creature whose victimization, whether from a life-denying father or a castrating woman, is not entirely undeserved.

This emphasis upon victimization is also present in the evocation of the childhood dream of Hell. But a new element in this dream provides us with additional insight into Feuermann's fascination with a past he abhors. The presence of a "chorus" whose lamentations accompany the child's ascents and descents among the icy circles of Hell introduces an element of pathos into the scene. The victim is not alone, and his terrible fate does not go unrecognized. The dream, then, in spite of the terror it evokes, represents a wish-fulfillment. Feuermann receives the sympathy that he feels he was denied in his childhood and which, as an adult, he cannot give himself. The unconscious processes of the dream-work reflect, and help explain, Feuermann's attraction to past which repells him: he must evoke his past in order to re-experience the punishment which his sense of guilt convinces him he deserves and, at the same time, seek the sympathy he feels he has been denied.

In Winter concludes, as do most autobiographical narratives, when the narrative of the past events converges upon the moment of writing. In this case, however, the convergence is of special significance, for it compels Feuermann to consider, once again, his relationship to his past and to his efforts to record it. He finally concludes that, although many more pages remain in his notebook, it would be futile to continue writing because he will never be able to "tell all." The winter drama of his life must always be marked, "to be continued." All the old fears and obsessions, the sense of irrevocable guilt and repulsion as well as the fatal attraction to self-analysis and doubt, remain. The only alternatives that Feuermann sees at this point are insanity or the "liberation" of suicide:

> In my Scripture now is found the following verse: See, before you lie two paths: the first involuntary, the second voluntary -- insanity or suicide. Now choose death! (58)

In the end, Feuermann pursues neither of these alternatives, but a kind of temporary liberation comes from an unexpected place:

> I am silent and I stop writing, that filthy labor. What was I thinking? I shall dash the cursed pen... (58)

Feuermann does not dash the pen (three more chapters remain to be written), but this expression of rage proves to be cathartic: for the moment, at least, he can look forward to the future as well as back to the past, and even see in that future cause for hope. "I know that the second half of my life will be completely different," he writes to his friend Davidovsky. "What do I have to do with probing scalpels?" Liberated for the moment from scalpel, if not pen, Feuermann can write the last chapters of his narrative (now more diary than autobiography) with an uncharacteristic stoic restraint and calm that are especially striking after the frantic introspection of the preceding chapters.

How can we describe this catharsis and the radical shift in tone that follows on its heels other than as an "event" in the narrating instance. Feuermann's recoiling from the act of narrating, expressed in his (unfulfilled) intention to dash his pen, is in fact no different in quality than the numerous other retractions and false starts, those traces of the narrating instance, that fill his narrative. The only difference here is that Feuermann, for the first time, directs his wrath not at himself, not at his own deficiencies, but at the act of writing itself. If earlier the problem was that his past was "gloomy and wretched," that he was a "non-hero," that lacked "art" to properly explain things, that his lust cannot be called "love," that he is stupid to use a "banal" term, here the problem is not in his past or in the type of man that past has made him, but in his present action, an action that, he now seems to discover for the first time, can be stopped. What

Feuermann discovers is that not only is his effort to "tell all" futile, it is also unnecessary. The "second half" of his life lies before him and it will be -- or so it appears to him at this point -- "completely different."

The catharsis, however, remains problematic and no doubt transitory. In the final entry of his autobiography-diary, Feuermann tells how he finds refuge from the wintery night -- and an anti-semitic station master -- under some timber piled behind a provincial train station on the way to the "second half" of his life. The imagery of winter has returned, and with it Feuermann's physical and spiritual isolation. Nothing has really been solved, no demons have been exorcised once and for all. Still, Feuermann's affirmation of the richness and complexity of life that "transcend all analysis," however ephemeral it may be, opens up possibilities which, while under the sway of the past, simply did not exist for him.

The apparent formlessness of the plots of Brenner's novels -- and particularly of In Winter -- has long been considered a weak point in his narrative art even by those who accepted it as a necessary though unfortunate corollary of his subject matter.[25] The plot of In Winter, however, appears formless only when it is analyzed according to conventional notions of plot structure, that is, when plot is viewed as a correlation of narrative units denoting actions in the narrated time and when the link between chronological and logical order is sought exclusively at that level. If, on the other hand, we approach the narrative units from the point of view of the narrating instance and consider them as acts of narration, another plot emerges whose regulating principle is neither logical nor chronological but rather psychological. The form of this plot is essentially cyclical and, at the most abstract level, can be reduced to four actions: (1) to remember, (2) to narrate, (3) to respond to the act of narration, and (4) to stop narrating. The first three actions, of course, constitute the cycle; the fourth action is the escape hatch, as it were, that brings the cycle to an end, and with it, the narrative itself. As we have seen, the cycle is reflected at all levels of the narrative, from the syntax of statement and retraction, to the organization and juxtaposition of larger narrative units, all the way to the global structure that pits the entire narrative, so to speak, against the statement "I will dash the cursed pen."

It is only by reference to this structure that the denouement of In Winter can be understood. For, as we have seen, this denouement does not take place in the narrated past; it is neither caused nor constituted by a specific event in Feuermann's "autobiography." Rather, it takes place in the narrating instance, at the moment when Feuermann, closed in by the inevitable convergence of narrated time and time of narration, turns his rage upon the act of writing and, as a result, "liberates" himself from his obsession with the past. Feuermann's need for such a liberation sets the narrative into motion; once achieved (even if temporarily), the narrative loses its raison d'être and grinds to a halt.

CHAPTER FIVE
Narrative as Psychological Drama:
Y.H. Brenner's Breakdown and Bereavement

In In Winter, Brenner captures the atmosphere of the mind of his protagonist by employing a first-person narrative mode in which the narrating instance -- the character of the narrator, the circumstances of his narration, his relation to what he narrates -- is the site of the novel's central drama. But fiction in which the atmosphere of the mind constitutes the primary object of representation is obviously not limited to a particular mode or voice. It is not the narrative mode itself that determines whether we are in the presence of psychological fiction, but the manner in which the chosen mode is exploited. While first-person narrative can, as in In Winter, present a profound and immediate impression of the inner conflicts of the narrator, it can also, as in Abramovitsh's The Beggars' Book, ignore or subvert the very notions of "character" and "psychological depth." Similarly, third-person narrative presents both advantages and disadvantages for psychological fiction. One advantage, clearly, is the ability of the narrator to "escape" the consciousness of the protagonist, something that is, of course, impossible in a first-person autobiographical narrative like In Winter. The third-person narrator can describe scenes and narrate events not witnessed by the protagonist, he can reveal the unspoken thoughts of other characters, and he can provide insight into the personality of the protagonist which might be beyond the protagonist's own powers of self-analysis. As a result, we are provided with apparently "objective" information about the protagonist and his environment according to which we can interpret and judge his perceptions and inner conflicts. A disadvantage of third-person narrative, on the other hand, is the potential lack of immediacy in the presentation of those inner conflicts. However unobtrusive the narrator may be, his presence always stands between the protagonist and the reader and thus sets us at a distance from the protagonist. If the narrator does obtrude by analyzing, summarizing, or evaluating the protagonist's thought world, the loss of immediacy may be considerable.

In his last and longest novel, Breakdown and Bereavement, Brenner makes full use of the advantages of third-person narrative. Indeed, the novel's protagonist, Yehezkel Hefetz, is virtually absent during long stretches of the narrative and plays only a marginal role in many of the novel's key events. Nevertheless, Brenner's presentation of Hefetz's inner conflicts loses none of the depth and immediacy he had achieved in the earlier novella. Those conflicts not only remain the central focus of the work, they dictate the nature and shape of the fictional world of Breakdown and Bereavement no less than the inner conflicts of Yermiah Feuermann had dictated the shape and nature of the fictional world of In Winter. In this chapter we will examine some of the techniques of third-person narrative that Brenner employs in order to expose the atmosphere of Yehezkel Hefetz's mind.

Breakdown and Bereavement opens with a preface in which a fictional editor describes how he came upon the notebooks that form the basis of the narrative that follows, and then goes on to apologize for the fact that, in spite of his best efforts to give the notebooks the "accepted and standard form of a story," many of the chapters still have the "odor of memoir." The editor's apology is clearly ironic, for Brenner's commitment to "authenticity" led him to expend great efforts to avoid the "accepted and standard" -- and therefore "inauthentic" -- forms of fiction.[1] By having his editor admit his "failure" to transform the notebooks into standard literary form, Brenner exposes and undercuts the conventions upon which that form is based and emphasizes the "authenticity" of the text.

Beyond the irony, however, Brenner also reveals the narrative technique that will enable him, in spite of the third-person narrative apparatus, to present the inner world of his protagonist with the same immediacy that can be achieved in first-person narratives. When the editor complains that in many passages one can still hear the "voice of one speaking on his own behalf in the third person," he is in fact describing a narrative technique through which psychological novelists using third-person narrative have excelled in exposing the atmosphere of the mind of their protagonists. Far from a flaw, as the editor would have us believe, Brenner's exploitation of this technique is perhaps his most impressive artistic achievement, and a key to the way in which the protagonist's inner world shapes the "external" world of the novel.

Here is a characteristic passage from the first chapter of Breakdown and Bereavement. Hefetz, on his way to Jerusalem with his friend Menahem after having suffered a hernia at an agricultural settlement in the north, recalls his first trip to Palestine, several years earlier:

> That trip, too -- why did it come about?... He had been about twenty years old when he came to Palestine; strong and healthy, undemanding, a bit odd perhaps, but respected. Elsewhere he had not been respected (in Himilin's circle of students, there, abroad, he had not been respected): a dull-witted, young man, slow, solemn, who did not know at all how to get along with young women, nor did they extend their favors to him -- in short, the very opposite of one worthy of respect... Yes, in another place someone like him could definitely not be respected! But at the worker's club in the settlement (...) there, only there, they could respect him, Hefetz, too.[2]

The question that opens this passage is not a rhetorical device used by the third-person narrator to introduce a conventional flashback. Nor are the conclusions that are drawn here those of an objective, "reliable" narrator. The question, the analysis it provokes, and the conclusions that are drawn are clearly those of Yehezkel Hefetz. This is clear not only from the highly subjective nature of that analysis, but from the style in which it is couched. Thus, for example, the large number of adjectives that crowd the first half of the passage (strong, healthy, undemanding, odd, respected, dull-witted, young, slow, solemn) and, in particular, the repetition of the word "respect" throughout the passage reflect Hefetz's obsessive concern with personal worth, especially in the eyes of others. The parenthetical intrusion through which Himilin is introduced reflects Hefetz's problematical relationship with the man whom he considers his sexual rival and nemesis. Throughout the novel Himilin shall continue to intrude upon Hefetz's thoughts, a focus of both attraction and repulsion. The punctuation used in the passage, the dashes and ellipses and the exclamation point that appears toward the end are the indices of thought in motion, rather than of static narrative summary or analysis. Thus, although grammatically the third person is maintained, we are, as it were, overhearing Hefetz's speech.

The voice we hear in this passage, then, is neither that of the narrator, summarizing the speech of the protagonist, nor the voice of the protagonist as we might get, for example, in direct speech or quoted internal monologue. Rather, the voice of the narrator and the voice of the protagonist merge, creating the narrative effect which the French call le style indirect libre, the German erlebte Rede, and for which Dorrit Cohn has more recently suggested the term, "narrated monologue."[3] The narrative statement, to use Mikhail Bakhtin's term, is "two-voiced": while we "hear" the voice of the protagonist in the content and style of the passage, the third-person form constantly reminds us of the hovering presence of the narrator.[4]

Examples of narrated monologue can be found in the literature of all ages, but it was only in the nineteenth century that its use became widespread, a development paralleling, to a large extent, the increasingly psychological concerns of the novel. The technique did not appear in the Hebrew novel, however, until late in the nineteenth century, and it was only in the works of Brenner and Gnessin at the beginning of the twentieth century that its potential was fully explored.[5] In their works, narrated monologue became a supple tool through which the constantly shifting perceptions, moods, and attitudes of their highly introspective protagonists were evoked with both subtlety and precision.

Narrated monologue makes possible the creation of a complex, highly nuanced and often ambiguous relationship between narrator and protagonist. Thus, the implicit tensions involved in the "two-voiced" statement can be exploited for ironic and satiric effects; the hovering narrative presence can provide a kind of counter-statement to the character's statement. On the other hand, the narrator's voice can merge with that of the character, providing corroboration or empathy. Characteristically, however, both aspects of narrated monologue exist side by side in a constantly shifting relationship in which now one, now the other, gains the upper hand. In Breakdown and Bereavement the satirical function of narrated monologue is reserved almost exclusively for secondary characters. With the protagonist, on the other hand, the tension between narrator and protagonist almost completely disappears, and the two voices often merge so thoroughly that it is virtually impossible to distinguish between the two. Thus, as in the passage we have analyzed, we indeed seem to hear the "voice of one speaking on his own behalf in the third person."

Such is the case, as well, when Himilin, Hefetz's European rival, shows up in Jerusalem, and Hefetz is forced to deal with him for a second time. An actual confrontation between the two never occurs, but Himilin's very presence in Jerusalem is enough to exacerbate Hefetz's abiding anxieties:

> To each his own, to Himilin, too. And yet the truth was that he hated him, hated him with a passion, had hated him ever since the incident at the widow's house. Why deny it? And he didn't deny either that his hatred had nothing pure or ideal about it, like the hatred that anyone honest might feel for a scoundrel; no, for the most part it was simply the product of his irrepressible envy. But what did it all prove? (159)

As in the previous example, Hefetz's state of mind is not simply reported by the narrator, but rendered through narrated monologue. Here, especially, it is the movement of Hefetz's thought that is captured. Thus, Hefetz's initial dismissal of Himilin ("To each his own...") is followed immediately by his admission that in fact he cannot dismiss Himilin or his feelings toward him ("And yet... Why deny it?"). After admitting his hatred (the word is repeated five times in the passage!), Hefetz attempts to analyze his feelings and ends up condemning not Himilin but himself and his own "irrepressible envy." Then, as if this conclusion were too much for his consciousness to bear, he once again dismisses Himilin and denies the significance of both his self-analysis and its conclusions ("But what did it all prove?"). Hefetz's conflicting attitudes toward Himilin (and toward himself), then, are presented as they clash and collide in Hefetz's own thought processes. In spite of the third-person grammatical form, the presence of the narrator is hardly felt.

But even when the narrator's presence is felt more strongly, it is often impossible to draw a clear line between his voice and that of the protagonist. Thus, after Hefetz (in a passage of quoted interior monologue) compares Himilin to a noose around his neck, the narrator, adopting Hefetz's metaphor, has this to say:

> And the noose was indeed eternal, unfrayed, well-greased. There were infrequent days, to be sure — his last days in the hospital, for example, when it had seemed to widen and loosen, as it were. More recently, however, Himilin has ceased entirely to be a real person in his eyes, one who lived in the Harel, played with the affections of the owner's daughter, if Shneirson was to be believed, and conversed with Henya about Montefiore's pipe. Instead he had turned into something abstract -- a Himilinoid substance that had stolen the Russian widow's daughter from his arms -- an almost hallucinatory nightmare. (158)

Neither the passage itself nor the context in which it appears allows us to determine whether the thoughts expressed here are those of the narrator or those of Hefetz. But even if this is an example of what Dorrit Cohn calls "psycho-narration" (reported as opposed to rendered thought), the very ambiguity points up the absolute consonance between the protagonist's and the narrator's point of view. For not only does the narrator take up and expand Hefetz's metaphor, he does so in language and syntax virtually indistinguishable from that of passages of unmistakable narrated monologue. Nor does the narrator describe Hefetz's state of mind (if that is in fact what we are dealing with) from a position of superior knowledge. While we are told that Himilin has ceased to be a "real person" in Hefetz's eyes (and there is no reason to believe that Hefetz himself is not aware of this), no effort is made to contrast the "real" Himilin with the "Himilinoid substance" that Hefetz's obsession has made of him.

Whether we are dealing with narrated monologue or psycho-narration, the object of Hefetz's inner conflicts (in this case Himilin) is not presented as it may appear to an "objective, clear-headed observer," but rather as a creature of Hefetz's consciousness, a "substance" to be shaped according to Hefetz's obsessions and fantasies. It is not surprising, then, that the only "confrontation" between Hefetz and Himilin takes place in Hefetz's imagination. Sitting at his desk in Goldmann's house one day, Hefetz overhears Himilin flirting in the next room with Henya, his employer's spoiled daughter. Abandoning his work, Hefetz imagines just what would transpire if he could engage Himilin in a philosophical debate. In the dialogue Hefetz concocts, Himilin declares the absolute value of instinctual fulfillment and the moral superiority of the strong and the beautiful over the weak. The so-called morality of the weak, Himilin declares, is simply the product of envy and a desire for revenge. In response, Hefetz defends the rights of the weak, not on the basis of their moral superiority, but simply because they, like the strong and the beautiful, maintain their will to live. "We, too, live," he states passionately, "we, too, have a portion in life" (141). It is pointless to wonder whether Himilin has read Nietzsche as passionately as Hefetz apparently has. Himilin has become an "abstract substance" to be molded according to Hefetz's obsessions. Whatever Himilin may really feel about such matters, for Hefetz he is the embodiment of Nietzsche's <u>Ubermensch</u>. And it is as such that Himilin plays a key role in the psychological drama at the heart of the novel.

Through the use of narrated monologue, then, Brenner not only captures the atmosphere of his protagonist's mind, he presents the fictional world and those who populate it as projections of Hefetz's consciousness. But narrated monologue is not the only technique through which a third-person narrator can transform the fictional world from objective reality to psychological landscape. Here, for example, is how Hefetz's cousins, Miriam and Esther, are described when we, and Hefetz, meet them for the first time in Jerusalem:

> Her [Miriam's] two braids, slipping from beneath the white scarf on her head, bobbed against the well-shaped shoulders visible beneath her sailor suit... her face tanned and pretty, if not finely featured, her dark blue flirtatious eyes flecked with a cat-like gray-green, the lines of her mouth fresh and attractive for all their stubborn, uninviting, unfeminine energy. The lively chatter of her speech, jumping from one thing to another, rose above the drone of the sewing machine and the plaintive hum of Esther, her pinched, wasted, sister, who sat singing softly over it. (52)

Although the description of the sisters is presented in the narrator's voice, it is focalized through Hefetz's point of view. The obsessional patterns of his perceptions dominate the passage. For Hefetz sexual attractiveness is always threatening, precisely because of the health and energy it suggests, and expects in return. Thus, along with her well-shaped shoulders, flirtatious eyes and attractive mouth, there is something vaguely threatening in the cat-like color of Miriam's eyes and her "stubborn, uninviting, unfeminine energy." On the other hand, Esther, stooped over her sewing machine, neither attracts nor threatens Hefetz. She is wilted and dried out, sickly like himself. Her plaintive hum contrasts sharply with the lively chatter of her sister.

The two sisters, then, are presented from the very beginning as objects of Hefetz's consciousness, and, as a result, the roles they play in his inner struggles are revealed from the outset. Miriam is to be the object of Hefetz's erotic desires, and thus unattainable and, at times, feared. Esther will become Hefetz's nurse and companion in suffering, but precisely because she shares and understands Hefetz's weakness, he will not be able to look upon her as a sexual partner. Later in the novel, this set of relationships is given concise symbolic expression in one of Hefetz's dreams. Hefetz finds himself in a field too weak to do the work required of him. Esther comes to the rescue:

> I'm on your side. Stay where you are, you're weak. Let me do the work. Just don't drink the groundwater. The water from Miriam's well is bitter, you'll get malaria... here, drink the milk that I've brought you. (82)

Esther comes to Hefetz's aid, offers to sacrifice herself for his good, and, in the process, attempts to "protect" him from Miriam's threatening sexuality. But Esther's aid contains a hidden threat. The milk she offers Hefetz not only suggests Hefetz's "maternal" view of her, it also conjures up the image of Yael who offered milk to Sisera only to kill him while he slept. Throughout the novel, Hefetz will resist Esther's sympathy, convinced that an acceptance of this kind of love would not only be hypocritical, but would mean the "death" of his erotic desires. Thus, just as Himilin, the model of health and uninhibited sexual energy, is transformed into an abstract "substance" in Hefetz's mind, Esther, who nurses Hefetz during both his physical and psychological crises, is seen finally as "some substantia of his deranged mind" (76), the embodiment of the weakness and "slave morality" that Hefetz sees in himself and which he feels he must flee at any cost.

Jerusalem, the city to which Hefetz comes in the hope of finding a cure for both his physical and his mental distress, does not escape this process of internalization and transformation. Like Himilin, Miriam and Esther, the city is swallowed up by Hefetz's all-consuming consciousness. As a result, it does not merely represent an autonomous, external reality, a "social background" to Hefetz's inner struggles. Descriptions of the blind cruelty of Jerusalem's institutions, its cynical public officials, ineffectual or simply hypocritical idealists and, above all, its many victims represent an extension of the inner struggle, a psychological landscape whose ultimate source must be sought in the act of perception itself. In the courtyard of the Jerusalem hospital in which he is being treated for his injury, Hefetz sees at close hand some of Jerusalem's insulted and injured:

> The sighs and complaints didn't cease for a moment. But the light Jerusalem breeze, blowing over the bare hilltops, scattered them all and turned them to naught, to a meaningless cipher. Here a poor woman evicted from her house, thrown into the street without even a bed... And there an old man about to die, his wife pining for him in the yard; a boy on fire with fever and his father

waiting on burning coals for his recovery, while his neighbor on the bench tried to comfort him with the thought that it was better to be dying than dead... (51)

Although it is the narrator's voice we hear, the scene, like the description of the sisters, is strictly mediated through Hefetz's point of view. It is Hefetz who hears the sighs and complaints that never cease, who witnesses the pain of those in the courtyard, and who notes the Jerusalem breeze that turns all to "naught, to a meaningless cipher." The reader "sees" the scene only insofar as it impinges upon Hefetz's consciousness, as it is internalized and transformed into an element of the inner struggle. As the narrator's voice merges with Hefetz's inner voice, it is precisely the inner struggle that dominates the passage:

Take them, too, you thieves, take them to the grave; What good to them is life... Oy, oy, oy... distress upon distress. And yet it aroused no feeling. Nothing. The breeze blew through the yard of the hospital, the stones lay idly by. The world was turned to stone. Stone. It was all one. He whom the evil had reached, let him suffer... And we? (31-2)

A world turned to stone, immobile, undifferentiated, lifeless, swept by a breeze that turns everything into a "meaningless cipher," this is the Jerusalem that Hefetz ultimately perceives. It is a world that both beckons to him and terrifies him, for to become part of it, Hefetz feels, would be to surrender to his own weaknesses, his own "guilt." When Hefetz exclaims ironically to his friend, Menahem, "Now I am a complete Jerusalemite," he is not referring to a geographical location or a social milieu, but to a state of mind, a psychological reality of which he is both the creator and the victim.

<u>Breakdown and Bereavement</u>, however, does not deal exclusively with the inner struggles of Yehezkel Hefetz, at least not directly. More than half of the novel, in fact, is devoted to the fate of Hefetz's uncles, Yosef and Haim, to the aimless existence of Shneirson and his friends, and to the petty intrigues of Goldmann and his cronies. Hefetz is often no more than a silent observer in these affairs, and at times he is not even present. In these cases, of course, it is the third-person, omniscient narrator who describes the scene, analyzes the characters, and interprets the action. Moreover, the narrator often dips into the thoughts of secondary characters and evokes <u>their</u> inner struggles through narrated monologue. Thus the fictional framework established in the preface -- i.e., that what we are reading is based upon Hefetz's notebooks -- is constantly violated. Moreover, we would seem to have access to an autonomous world beyond Hefetz's consciousness against which we can measure his subjective perceptions.

This autonomy, however, is more apparent than real. For in Hefetz's absence, the narrator serves, in effect, as his proxy, bringing Hefetz's attitudes, sympathies, and obsessions to bear even upon situations and events which he does not or cannot witness. As Hefetz's proxy, the narrator clearly directs the reader's sympathies, at times with a rather heavy hand. Thus, characters whom Hefetz finds objectionable or ridiculous are treated with obvious contempt by the narrator and often become the victims of sharp, bitter irony. Conversely, characters with whom Hefetz shares a common sense of victimization, such as his uncles, Yosef and Haim, escape such ironic judgment. Even when they themselves are partially responsible for their ordeals, the narrator treats them with deference and empathy.

Here, for example, is how the narrator introduces Shneirson, the smug pseudo-intellectual whose opinionated speeches Hefetz must endure during his stay at his uncle's house:

> Shneirson, Miriam's tutor, was a young Hebrew nationalist, certainly no worse than any of his Russian friends and contemporaries who had debarked at one time or another off the coast of Palestine's Jaffa. They admired the splendid scenery from the deck of the ship, went into town feeling dreadfully moved, lost their temper at the Arabs who approached them on the way, ordered their meals at the hotel, told tales about the local farmers who weren't hiring Jewish workers, went out to work one morning with a hoe on their shoulder and a bottle of water and half a loaf of bread tucked under their arm, wandered about the settlements, made the pilgrimage to Jerusalem for one of the holidays, looked forward to seeing the Galilee, and when they were through tramping about -- ended up with some trivial post as a secretary or teacher in Jaffa or Jerusalem. (69)

Shneirson is reduced here to a type, a representative "young Hebrew nationalist," rather than an individual with a unique history and set of aspirations. He is "no worse" than his friends and contemporaries and, for that matter, not very different. Thus, rather than describing Shneirson himself, the narrator goes on to describe the type, presenting in broad satirical terms a kind of communal biography of high expectations and minimal results. Even as he stagnates in Jerusalem, Shneirson continues to expound his "ideals," losing no opportunity to harangue all who will listen concerning the urgent need for Jewish cultural and national revival. The satirical judgment here is unambiguous. The narrator surveys Shneirson from a distance, places him in a clearly defined category, and then exposes the wide gap between romantic ideals and unpleasant reality which Shneirson either cannot or will not acknowledge.

When such characters speak, the manner in which the narrator renders their speech is calculated to reveal their hypocrisy. We are told that when Shneirson would meet a female acquaintance:

> he would avoid, on the surface, speaking to her at all, yet, in the end, he would be called upon and would speak on silence, which is greater than words, and would not, when necessary, fail to mention what we find in Maeterlinck or some other poet. From here, he would move on to his impressions from Europe from two years before. There he did not fail to notice this and that. Now he sits in the Harel and doesn't see a thing. Even though, in truth, that hotel is an arena of types. Does she understand? It seems to him that this says it all. (71)

Although the manner in which this passage slides from narrative commentary to narrated monologue is similar to passages we have analyzed involving Hefetz, the purpose to which this technique is put here could hardly differ more. In Hefetz's case, as we have seen, the narrative voice merges with that of Hefetz to the point that the two are virtually indistinguishable. Thus there is little room for irony, much less overt narrative judgment. Here, however, the narrator's voice maintains its independent presence and perspective, and if it adopts elements of Shneirson's overblown speech, it does so only to deflate it. Indeed, the narrator drains Shneirson's speech of any real content it may have originally had, leaving only an empty shell of intellectual pretension. It makes no difference whether Shneirson mentions Maeterlinck or "some other poet," or what precisely it was that he "did not fail to notice" in Europe. Shneirson's overriding concern is to make an impression, to display what he considers his superior intellect and sensitivity. By adopting yet sabotaging Shneirson's unremitting cant, this is exactly what the narrator reveals. The two "voices" of narrated monologue are clearly operative here. Though sometimes submerged, the narrator's voice supplies an ironic counterpoint to the character's speech, exposing, now explicitly, now implicitly, the latter's hypocrisy.

The narrator's contempt for Hefetz's "enemies" -- the sexual rival Himilin, the pseudo-intellectual Shneirson, among others -- is never disguised and seldom subtle. With irony, sarcasm, invective, and mimicry, he seems to delight in exposing their sins and follies. Goldmann, the self-serving "public servant" who causes so much hardship for Yosef and Haim, comes in for particularly harsh treatment, as does his "bourgeois" household:

> Despite the expense of doing business in Jerusalem, Goldmann's household lacked for nothing. There were tender grilled birds, fish fresh from the Jordan, bottles of wine with genuine labels, all kinds of sweets and desserts; there were quantities of linen and silver, furniture from the workshop of the German cabinetmaker, pearl necklaces in little cases; there were "social calls" and pleasant conversation, accompanied all day by sips of coffee, concerning houses, marriages, the price of goods -- in a word, whatever people of the world discuss in their leisure hours, the men seeking to turn the talk to some modest theoretical conclusion, their hostesses cutting them short time and again with an unconsciously impatient "yes, but..." to continue the chatter unchallenged and uninterrupted by themselves. It was a house that had everything -- everything one could desire. Just one thing is missing, Yehezkel Hefetz thought, one thing alone that this house has never known, which it would be almost impolite to name: a bit of real laughter. Of such there was none in his uncle's house, none in the guesthouse chapel, but least of all was there any in Goldmann's own house... (152)

The Goldmann household embodies, according to the narrator, all the worst aspects of materialistic bourgeois culture. It is a house that has "everything one could desire," as long as one's desires are limited to physical satisfaction, primarily in the form of fancy foods, luxury items, and the insipid conversation of "social calls." It is the great "thesis and anti-thesis" of bourgeois culture, as enunciated by Goldmann's mother, that reigns here: "This is practical; this is not practical." Thus, when these "people of the world" gather to discuss the affairs to the day, their conversation is limited to "houses, marriages, and the price of goods." The narrator surveys all this with undisguised contempt, and then goes on to expose Goldmann's corrupt dealings, the childish greed of Henya, his spoiled daughter, and the more mature and earnest avarice of his mother.

Hefetz and the narrator are not only in complete agreement in their evaluation of the Goldmann household, they collaborate, as it were, in exposing its "true" nature. Thus, the irony in the narrator's statement that the Goldmann household "lacked for nothing" is made explicit by Hefetz's reference to what in fact the household does lack: human warmth in the form of a "bit of real laughter." To this comment, the narrator voices his agreement and then goes on to explore the implications of this "fact." Clearly, then, the narrator does not provide us with an "objective" view of the Goldmann household against which we can measure and evaluate Hefetz's perceptions. As in the case of Shneirson, the narrator adopts Hefetz's attitudes and values and uses them to generate his satiric portrait of the "bourgeois household." If the narrator describes that household as a stronghold of corrupt bourgeois values, it is because Hefetz sees it as such.

As in In Winter, the inner life of the protagonist of Breakdown and Bereavement -- whether presented through narrated monologue or psycho-narration, or reflected in focalized description or the narrator's function as proxy -- determines the shape and nature of the fictional world. That world is a projection of the protagonist's consciousness, his obsessions, his inner conflicts, his attitudes and values. Therefore, as in the earlier novel, the narrated events and descriptions of setting can only be properly analyzed as indices of the protagonist's "character," and thus as elements of the drama that takes place in his mind. And as in the earlier novel, this drama revolves around a transformation in the protagonist's inner world, a change in the atmosphere of his mind. In In Winter, that atmosphere was dominated by the protagonist's obsession with an "unheroic" past, his sexual failings, and the very possibility of narrating the story of his life. In Breakdown and Bereavement, ideology and philosophy mingle with similar obsessions to create a more complex atmosphere of the mind and, as a result, a more complex transformation whose dynamics we must trace before we can consider the effect that that transformation has on the presentation of the fictional world.

Hefetz's (and the narrator's) attitude toward Shneirson and the Goldmann household is based in part on a set of values adhered to by many protagonists of modern fiction. These "modern spiritual heroes," as Lionel Trilling has called them, characteristically reject the "specious good" of bourgeois culture and seek instead a higher, more spiritual existence, even though the means they use to accomplish this goal are often perverse and self-destructive.[6] They have nothing but contempt for what they consider the bourgeoisie's unbridled devotion to the pleasure principle, its all-embracing concern with material comfort, physical gratification, and amusement. But it is not merely the outward manifestations of bourgeois culture that Hefetz objects to. Hefetz's most bitter diatribes are reserved for the ideologists of the bourgeois faith, the "priests of the beautiful, the heroes of the harmoniousness." (26) For Hefetz, they are guilty of intellectual bad faith, for with their pretense of reason and objectivity they attempt to legitimize a way of life that ignores the harsh reality of the modern world, particularly the modern world of the Jew. In a world of social and cultural disintegration, a world that has lost God and, as a result, can provide no meaning for suffering and death, they merely raise false hopes. Worse, through their willingness to compromise with half-truths, they encourage the hypocrisy of the Goldmanns, the self-deception of the Shneirsons.

Unlike the "priests of harmony," Hefetz is driven to confront the worst implications of his own (and, by extension, the human) predicament with a "clear head." He must constantly probe, analyze, evaluate his own inclinations and motives, subject himself to harsh, often morbid self-criticism in an attempt to arrive at a "true account." He refuses to deceive himself, to compromise or accept partial but comforting answers to the questions and doubts that plague him. Most of all, he feels he must face squarely his own failures and weaknesses, his sense of inferiority, guilt, and ultimately, the "void within." Toward the end of <u>Breakdown and Bereavement</u>, Hefetz is still trying to arrive at a "true account," and his efforts lead him to one inescapable conclusion:

> No, no more brave words, no more running away from the true account. If God had created him twisted, was he any the less accountable? Enough brave words. When things are grim, black, hopeless, impossible, why pervert the plain facts with bravado, with the high-flown bluster that stupid, self-indulgent little men -- and sometimes even not such little men -- spouted on every street corner? He, at least, knew his own self. And he had no illusions about the fact that he was beaten. In every way a beaten man. (296)

This intense and constant self-evaluation and stubborn insistence on the "true account" prompted F. Lahover to characterize the stance of Brenner's protagonists as a "heroism of the truth."[7] It is a particularly tragic heroism, since the attempt to face the truth with a clear head inevitably leads Hefetz to the realization of his utter defeat by life and, like so many of Brenner's protagonists, to mental breakdown and serious contemplation of suicide. But, as Natan Zach has correctly pointed out, the "sickness" of Brenner's heroes is, paradoxically, their very strength.[8] For it is only by getting beyond the pleasure principle, by <u>making</u> himself vulnerable, that the modern spiritual hero attains the spiritual existence he demands. Thus, like Dostoyevsky's Underground Man, Hefetz might claim in the end that:

> all I did was carry to the limit what you haven't dared to push even half way -- taking your cowardice for reasonableness, thus making yourselves feel better. So I may still turn out to be more alive than you in the end.[9]

For Hefetz, being "more alive" means finally accepting "what is," and learning how to affirm all of life for the sake of the few precious moments of relief, even happiness, that life can offer even the most wretched individual. This affirmation begins with Hefetz's realization that there is no transcendent or ethical meaning to his "defeat," and his stoic acceptance of this fact. Hefetz expresses this view of life, and the stoic resignation it requires, in a parable:

> Listen. A rock fell down in a cave-in. A heavy rock. It fell on a dog's head. A lethal blow. He never stood a chance. He took one last great jump, let out one last great howl. But he wasn't a stupid dog. Dogs are smarter than you think. His eyes, his cloudy dog's eyes, stayed calm. He didn't jump or howl

> any more. He didn't even think of biting anyone. Bite them? He couldn't
> even see them. Even the cave-in was forgotten. Even the rock. Hurrah for
> life. Hurrah for breath. Cooly, collectedly, he hobbled bleeding back to his
> hole. Spider webs. A quiet place to lie down. For a few more hours, a few
> more days, even a few more years -- he'll lie there and be still. (288-9)

However chilling this parable may be, it is the key to Hefetz's ultimate affirmation of life. For it is only by accepting life as it presents itself to the terminal victim that one can make the one affirmation that, for Hefetz, is authentic. The dog in the parable is not stupid because he knows how to accept his ordeal calmly and place ultimate value on the few hours, days or years of life and breath that remain for him. The "hurrah for life" rings true only when it is coupled with an acute awareness of life's negation.

The psychological drama of <u>Breakdown and Bereavement,</u> then, ends with the protagonist's affirmation of the "existing content of life," an affirmation achieved only after an arduous inner struggle in which the inevitability and meaninglessness of suffering and death are never lost sight of. What is especially significant for us, however, is that as soon as Hefetz reaches this state of affirmation, the fictional world of the novel undergoes a virtual transfiguration. Hefetz and his uncle's household abandon the harried atmosphere of Jerusalem for the serenity of Tiberias, but this move does not involve simply a shift from one social milieu to another. The change in atmosphere has little to do with the change of place itself. It is the narrator's voice, now calm, peaceful, and elegiac, that accomplishes this transformation by echoing Hefetz's new state of mind as he describes the Tiberias landscape:

> The evening was calm and dry. The trickle of moonbeams from above was like
> a last reflection of the afterglow of the sun as it fell away from the lakeside,
> the glow which seemed to come from so far off and left a special sense of
> peacefulness behind it. Still afire with a reddish play of stone, the chain of
> harp-shaped hills that ringed the city made its unspoken-of presence felt in the
> streets below. (302)

This is not a description of an objective social reality but one more psychological landscape. In place of the Jerusalem of distress and despair, a world that had turned to stone and which presents nothing but a meaningless cipher, the Tiberias landscape is full of evocative distances, special senses, and unspoken-of presences. It is a world suffused with the serenity of stoic acceptance whose source, though he is neither the observer nor the observed here, is Yehezkel Hefetz.

Tiberias, with its long-suffering but pious inhabitants and its healing hot springs ("When the pain is great," one of the inhabitants remarks, "it is a sign that the waters are healing.") represents, then, an external symbolic analogue to Hefetz's new state of mind. All the events that occur in and around Tiberias in the closing chapters of the novel conform to Hefetz's new "vision" of life. Menahem, the free-spirited wanderer who, from the very beginning, knew instinctively how to accept the "existing content of life," reappears, and his laughter "rolls over the banks of the Kinneret and is answered by an echo from the mountains." (295) Yosef repents his former severity and comes to the realization that if the world is at times like a raging sea, as his books tell him, it can also be like the tranquil Kinneret near whose banks he now lives. And Haim, whose constant struggle to eke out an existence for himself and his brother's family in Jerusalem never dulled his zest for life, experiences a sudden feeling of well-being as he watches, from the shores of the Kinneret, a group of Bedouin swimmers in the distance. "He who fears the water," he muses, "does not drown. Take Yosef, for example... or himself... people like them never drown. People like them kept alive" (310). Finally, the thought of bringing Haim's orphaned grandson from Jerusalem fills Haim and Yosef, and especially Yehezkel, with the hope that better days are about to arrive. It was, indeed, the orphan's simple acceptance of life's "moments of light, warmth, and sun" that Hefetz witnessed in the Jerusalem orphanage which provided him, "the orphan of orphans," with a model for his affirmation of life.

As in In Winter, the affirmation of life that brings the psychological drama of Breakdown and Bereavement to an end is not unequivocal. The fact that, as Haim sees it, people like the Hefetz's stay alive because they fear the water suggests that the affirmation involves, paradoxically, a retreat from life, at least as life is lived in Jerusalem. Moreover, the boat that Haim sees in the distance as he gazes over the waters of the Kinneret recalls the boat upon which the "editor" discovered the notebooks that form the basis of the novel and, moreover, where Hefetz apparently committed suicide. Nevertheless, Hefetz's affirmation of life, however problematic and transitory, has, at least for the moment, engendered a new world.

The central drama of Breakdown and Bereavement, no less than that of In Winter, is a psychological drama involving the inner conflicts and ultimate affirmation of the protagonist. Were we to attempt to analyze or even schematize the plot of either novel as a series of events and their "syntactic" relations, we would, at best, come up with a greatly impoverished description of little relevance to the novels themselves, but more likely an aggregate of units for which we could discover neither wholeness nor a principle of self-regulation. For the regulating principle of the narrative structure of these novels is neither logical nor chronological but rather psychological. The signification of the narrative units and the wholeness of the structure they form can only be discovered by reference to the character whose consciousness constitutes the structure's regulating principle. Clearly, any theory of narrative that ignores or discounts "character" can provide little insight into narratives in which the "character" of the protagonist plays such a crucial structural role.

CHAPTER SIX

Man and Dog in S.Y. Agnon's Only Yesterday

In the previous chapters we dealt with works that represent extreme poles on the continuum that stretches between a-psychological fiction and psychological fiction. In Abramovitsh's The Beggars' Book, the "character" of Mendele, the narrator-hero, is subordinated and ultimately subverted by the author's thematic concerns and the local needs of the narrative. In the case of Brenner's novels, not only do Yermiah Feuermann and Yehezkel Hefetz display coherent "characters," those characters constitute the regulating principles of the overall narrative structures in which they appear. Plot, setting, theme, and symbolic patterns, as indices of character, are constantly subordinated to the psychological drama.

The novel we shall now consider, S.Y. Agnon's Only Yesterday, belongs to that large class of "intermediary forms" that stand somewhere between the purely a-psychological and the emphatically psychological. Unlike Abramovitsh, Agnon provides the reader with enough information to draw a relatively coherent "semic portrait" of his protagonist. Unlike Brenner's protagonists, however, the inner life of Agnon's protagonist does not dominate or shape the fictional world. On the contrary, it is only one element of the fictional world that Agnon's third-person narrator presents, at times sympathetically, at times with sharp satire and irony. Thus, as in the case of most classically realistic novels, the relationship between the "character" of the protagonist of Only Yesterday (his semic portrait based upon a certain ideology of character) and the other elements of the narrative structure is, in Barthes' term, "undecidable." Even as he manifests a certain degree of individuality and free will, the protagonist conforms to the requirements of the narrative in which he participates. Or, as Benjamin Hrushovski would put it, the semantic units that we link up in order to realize the character of the protagonist are suspended in a network of hierarchies that constantly shifts according to the local requirements of the text or the interests of the reader.

Our task in analyzing the role of the protagonist in Only Yesterday, then, is not simply to determine and define his "character," but rather to show how that character and the manner in which it is revealed by the third-person narrator function in relation to the other elements of the narrative structure. What, in other words, is the precise nature of the undecidable relationship between character, plot, theme, and symbol in Only Yesterday?

Our task is complicated by the appearance of a second protagonist in Only Yesterday, a Jerusalem street dog named Balak. Balak emerges as a "character" no less than does the human protagonist of the novel, Yitshak Kummer. Indeed, the dog's inner life is, if anything, presented with greater detail and depth than that of Kummer. The question we must answer, then, is why, about halfway through an otherwise realistic novel, Agnon chose to introduce a fabulistic narrative which, from that point on, unfolds alongside the realistic narrative, whose plot bears unmistakable parallels to that narrative, and whose protagonist is a highly introspective dog passionately devoted to truth? More specifically, what limitations in his human protagonist prompted Agnon to introduce a second, canine protagonist? What function does Balak serve in the novel? Why cannot Yitshak fulfill that function? Why can Balak?

* * *

For a novel that deals, at least ostensibly, with what is conventionally viewed as the heroic period of Zionist settlement in Palestine, Yitshak Kummer is a disconcertingly unheroic hero. He is a thoroughly mediocre figure, quite passive by nature, and seemingly incapable of self-reflection or analysis. Moved only by vague desires and good intentions, Yitshak is unable to confront or even recognize the forces that frustrate his desires and subvert his ideals. Thus, his actions, when not simply the product of reflex or inertia, are typically ill-considered and lead, more often than not, to results the implications of which he seldom understands or pursues. Yitshak, Agnon's narrator insists, is not even an interesting character:

> Yitshak did not make an impression on people. There are many young men like Yitshak, and one does not pay much attention to them. Yitshak excelled in neither looks nor conversation. If you happened to speak with him, you would not be enthusiastic about speaking with him again. If you met him in the market place several times, you still would not recognize him. With a youth like Yitshak, if you were not particularly fond of him you treated him as though he did not exist.[1]

While Yitshak is in no way exceptional, his decision to come to Palestine certainly is. From the very first lines of the novel, however, the narrator makes it clear that while Yitshak may be an idealist, he is also extremely naive. Thus, after evoking the messianic images of pastoral harmony and prosperity that Yitshak imagines he will find in Palestine ("In the evening, each man would sit under his own vine, under his own fig tree, while his wife and sons and daughters sat around him, happy in their labor and joyful in their rest..."[2]), the narrator tells us rather bluntly that Yitshak is a "dreamer" and that his visions of the Land of Israel are really nothing more than a collection of fantasies. Nevertheless, bolstered by Zionist slogans and messianic fantasies, Yitshak sets off for Palestine, expecting to have little trouble joining the pioneers in their struggle to rebuild the Land. Yitshak is the innocent from the provinces, and because of his innate optimism and good will he accepts uncritically the hypocrisy and corruption of values with which he is, more often than not, confronted. Thus, passing through Lemberg on his journey to Palestine, he is impressed and inspired by a group of professional Zionist activists who treat him with bemused condescension and provide him with a perfectly meaningless letter of introduction to the leaders of the <u>yishuv</u>. Yitshak does not notice that even as they mouth the slogans of national revival in Palestine they clearly prefer the comfort and luxury that only the urban centers of Europe can offer. Once in Palestine, Yitshak falls easy prey to an unscrupulous innkeeper in Jaffa, and when he finally makes it into the countryside, he is rebuffed by the Jewish plantation owners who prefer cheap, experienced Arab labor to that of "dangerous" Zionists like himself.

Yitshak accepts his disappointments with cheerful equanimity, always confident that sooner or later he will begin building the Land. Even when he drifts back to Jaffa and hears the bitter complaints of the "veterans," Yitshak cannot be disillusioned or embittered. Yitshak's nature is to flow with the tide and, thus, when he is mistaken for a house painter in Jaffa, he accepts the job offered him and ends up with an emphatically urban trade. Giving himself over to the pleasures of a relatively prosperous bachelor life in Jaffa, he hardly seems to notice that he has abandoned his original reason for coming to Palestine.

Eventually, however, Yitshak is attacked by doubts and anxieties. He is disturbed by his haphazard abandonment of religious observance, his family's poverty back home in Galicia (to which the expense of his trip to Palestine contributed), and his sexual misadventure with Sonya, a liberated Jaffa type. These pangs of remorse and guilt, however, are always short-lived and never lead to action. Yitshak's power of introspection is notably weak, and he is easily distracted from painful thoughts. It is only after he visits Petah Tikva, a successful Zionist agricultural settlement, that Yitshak is reminded of his failure to settle on the Land. No longer satisfied with his life in Jaffa, he sets out for Jerusalem, not at all sure of what he will find there or, for that matter, of what it is he is seeking.

Yitshak's adventures in Palestine, then, eventually bring him back to his point of departure, the world of tradition which he had abandoned in order to fulfill his Zionist dreams. After some time in Jerusalem, Yitshak gravitates toward Meah Shearim, the stronghold of traditional religious life in the Holy City. He is befriended by the pious Moshe Amram whom he had met earlier on the boat to Palestine, lets his beard grow, begins to frequent the synagogues, and eventually courts Moshe Amram's granddaughter, Shifra, whose father is the well known fanatic, Reb Fayash. But Meah Shearim is only a twisted and distorted version of the world of tradition. It is dominated by Reb Fayash whose fanaticism had discredited him in Europe and by Reb Gronam Yekum Purkan whose grotesque fire and brimstone sermons transfix the crowds that flock to hear him. The two truly pious figures of the novel, Moshe Amram and Reb Alter, the mohel from Yitshak's home town, keep their distance from the communal life of the quarter.

Nor is Yitshak destined to find refuge in this deceptively familiar world. His Galician origins, his worldly trade, and especially his Zionist background make Yitshak suspect in the eyes of the inhabitants of Meah Shearim. Even after his marriage to Shifra, which was carefully avoided by the "pious," Yitshak's social ostracism continues. He seems destined to be an eternal outsider until, standing one day at the edge of a crowd listening to one of Reb Yekum Purkan's sermons, he is attacked by a mad dog. After a week of terrible pain he dies.

The narrator's attitude toward Yitshak is a curious mixture of empathy and deprecation. Although he typically refers to Yitshak as "our comrade," he seems intent upon keeping him at arm's length and seldom passes up an opportunity to point out his deficiencies. Here, for example, is how the narrator evokes Yitshak's uneasiness over his abandonment of religious observance and his "affair" with Sonya:

> Although Yitshak did not come to the Land of Israel for the sake of Torah and prayer, like that old man he had met on the boat and like so many other old men, still, he was sorry that his faith had weakened. Had his faith not weakened, he would not have done what he did. And since he recalled what he had done, he recalled Sonya. In truth, he did not take his mind off Sonya for even an hour, but he erred in thinking that he thought of her only because he wanted to correct his behavior toward her. (164)

After a summary statement noting Yitshak's sorrow over his "weakened faith," the narrator shifts briefly to <u>le style indirect libre</u> as Yitshak makes the connection between this weakening and his affair with Sonya ("Had his faith not weakened..."). The narrative voice, however, at once returns to report the immediate movement of Yitshak's thought ("And since he recalled what he had done...") and then Yitshak's general state of mind ("In truth, he did not take his mind off Sonya..."). Then, adding his superior judgement to his omniscience, the narrator calls attention to Yitshak's self-deception. Yitshak may believe that his intentions are pure, but the narrator knows better.

The narrator's criticism of Yitshak, however, is usually qualified by sympathetic understanding. If Yitshak fails to live up to his ideals or to come to grips with his failures, it is not the result of willful self-deception or hypocrisy on his part. Yitshak's failures, the narrator insists, are simply the result of his mediocrity. Thus, after describing a moment in which Yitshak finds release from his feelings of guilt through prayer ("Yitshak forgot all his guilt and appeared in his eyes like a child who has never sinned..."), the narrator goes on to explain why, for Yitshak, such "grace" can only be temporary:

> But grace does not last, for it is the way of grace to appear only from time to time, especially to a man who is not worthy of having the light of grace shine upon him without interruption. No matter how much we attempt to speak in Yitshak's favor, we must admit that he was no better than the rest of our comrades. What is there to say? We all seek the good, but the good which we seek is not the true good. (263)

Yitshak may not be worthy of uninterrupted grace, but this is so only because he is no better than the "rest of our comrades." Yitshak fails to seek the true good, but of this, the narrator insists, we are all guilty.

Beneath the narrator's often critical and at times condescending attitude, then, there is a fundamental sympathy for his naive and often foolish protagonist. Moreover, the narrator often displays a certain reticence in analyzing Yitshak's inner life, a reticence that leads him, at times, to adopt a kind of selective omniscience. Here, for example, is how the narrator "analyzes" the reasons behind Yitshak's decision to leave Jaffa, the site of his many failures, for Jerusalem:

> Yitshak returned to work, or rather, let's be honest, he did not return to work but to a life of idleness. Before his visit to Petah Tikva, Sonya was the cause of his idleness; after he returned from Petah Tikva, other causes came. Whatever the case, Yitshak realized that here it was not good for him and that he had to go somewhere else. (181)

The narrator knows that Yitshak's preoccupation with Sonya was the cause of his idleness before his trip to Petah Tikva. As for his idleness after the trip, however, he seems less certain, or at least less willing to confide in the reader, and thus hedges by simply referring to "other causes" without offering any further explanation. Indeed, the narrator seems to suggest that such explanation is irrelevant and that it is enough for us simply to know that Yitshak felt he had to "go somewhere else." This equivocation on the part of the narrator works at least two ways. On the one hand, it intimates the unconscious and overdetermined nature of Yitshak's motives. At the same time, however, by refusing to reveal or analyze those motives, and even suggesting their irrelevance, it undermines the classically realistic notion of "character" as a moral agent whose unity of being is reflected in his action.

Yitshak's status as a "character" in the classical sense is further eroded by the narrator's intentional obfuscation -- indeed, his near-denial -- of a cause-and-effect relationship between intention and action in his description of the first confrontation between Yitshak and the novel's other protagonist, Balak. Yitshak is painting a building on the outskirts of Meah Shearim when Balak, seeking water in the drought-stricken city, is attracted to Yitshak's moist brush. At first, Yitshak tries to drive the dog away, but when Balak persists, he ends up painting the words "mad dog" on Balak's back. Here is how the narrator describes the moment:

> Yitshak took one of his brushes, but he did not know whether he meant to threaten the dog with it or if he meant to wipe it on the dog's coat... Yitshak's arm stretched out and his hands began to tremble... He extended the paint brush toward the dog and the dog extended himself toward Yitshak... We do not know whether he originally intended to write what he wrote, or if in the end it merely seemed to him that he wrote it on purpose. But why should we involve ourselves with doubtful things? Better we should observe his action. (275)

The indeterminacy of Yitshak's thought processes ("... but he did not know whether...") is here matched by the narrator's own equivocation and ultimate disclaimer of special knowledge ("We do not know whether..."). As in the previous passage, the narrator momentarily abdicates his role as omniscient narrator and, instead, adopts the stance of an outside observer who can only speculate about Yitshak's intentions. And as before, the narrator finally admits his impatience with such speculation ("But why should we involve ourselves with doubtful things?").

By refusing to speculate about "doubtful things" and urging that we do the same, the narrator suggests not only that the ultimate source of Yitshak's behavior cannot be easily ascertained, but that it is largely irrelevant to the story he is telling. Indeed, for all the narrator reveals about Yitshak, there remains a gap in his character, an area to which we have no access and for which the narrator sees no reason to provide access. Yitshak's "refusal" to part with his innocence and naivete, his utter passivity in the face of the social, cultural and historical upheavals that surround him, and the docility with which he allows circumstance and chance to determine his fate are left, finally, unexplained.

* * *

In spite of the emphasis I have placed on the presentation of Yitshak Kummer, Only Yesterday is by no means simply the story of one man's fate. On the contrary, Yitshak's story is embedded in a sweeping evocation of the Second Aliyah and it is clear that one of Agnon's goals in writing the novel was to capture the unique atmosphere of this special historical moment. Thus, the historical and social setting of the novel is highly articulated and encompasses the major centers of Jewish settlement in Palestine. Yitshak's story is periodically interrupted by historical anecdotes describing the struggles and triumphs of the early Zionist pioneers, while satirical passages and vignettes poke fun at the inflated claims and hypocrisy that Yitshak often encounters as he attempts to realize his ideals. There is, moreover, an abundance of local color and numerous lyrical descriptions of town and country. A host of secondary characters -- pioneers, uprooted intellectuals, pious farmer and religious fanatics, artists, artisans, politicians, including a few well-known historical figures -- weave their way through the novel.

Underlying and giving shape to this profusion of historical and quasi-historical detail is Agnon's familiar concern with the relationship between tradition and modernity. As Arnold Band points out, the action of the novel oscillates between two "emotional and ideational poles" -- "modern" Jaffa with its Zionist pioneers and politicians, on the one hand, and "traditional" Jerusalem with its quiet pietists and more vocal fanatics.[3] As Yitshak himself oscillates between these poles, he encounters a wide variety of stances toward the past. Thus, in the Zionist milieu of Jaffa, he shares the life-style (if not the ideological platform) of the pioneers who attempt to escape tradition and the "galut mentality" by devoting themselves to the most crude forms of physical labor, hears speeches in which Zionism is held up as the path to the political and social normalization of the Jewish people, listens intently as Y.H. Brenner expounds upon the physical and spiritual regeneration to be derived from working the soil, and listens, as well, when Zionism is portrayed as a modern permutation of Jewish tradition, a kind of secular messianism. In Jerusalem, on the other hand, Yitshak is moved by the calm, traditional piety of Moshe Amram and Reb Alter, witnesses at close hand the fanaticism of Reb Fayash whose chief weapons against encroaching secularism are spiritual terror and excommunication, and is even attracted to the fire and brimstone sermons of Reb Gronam Yekum Purkan and his uncompromising denunciations of the "sinful generation."

Pointedly, the only person whom Yitshak meets who succeeds in bridging the gulf between tradition and modernity, Menahem, belongs to neither Jerusalem nor Jaffa. But Menahem is an exceptional and rather lonely figure. For Yitshak, who is often lonely but never exceptional, Menahem's solution is clearly beyond reach.

Indeed, Yitshak hardly seems to be aware of the existence of that gulf and, in any case, has neither the ability nor the inclination to consider, for example, distinctions between traditional and secular messianism. Yitshak came to Palestine with Zionist slogans and prophetic visions of the messianic age neatly fused in his mind, and his experiences in Palestine, rather incredibly, do nothing to sunder this naive synthesis. As a result, Jaffa, for all its liveliness and élan, fails to provide the spiritual security he needs. And while Jerusalem seems to offer that sense of security, it cannot make him forget his failure to live up to his Zionist ideals.

Caught thus between two worlds, Yitshak would seem to have much in common with the familiar figure of the talush, or "uprooted man" of turn-of-the-century Hebrew fiction. But if Yitshak belongs to the talush family, he is a poor relation indeed. In the works of Berdyczweski, Fierberg, and Brenner, for example, the talush boldly confronts his fate of homelessness, fully aware of the price he must pay for his spiritual and intellectual integrity. And while his quest is doomed to failure, the single-mindedness with which he pursues it endows him with heroic stature. The death or madness with which these stories typically conclude is the inevitable denouement of a heroic struggle with an implacable fate. Yitshak, on the other hand, is an innocent bystander, at most only partially responsible for his fate and not at all aware of the stakes involved in the struggle which, in any case, he does not pursue. Nor does Yitshak's death carry the significance that we associate with the death of the talush. Rather than a tragic apotheosis, it is a sudden intrusion into an aimless life gone awry.

While the earlier Hebrew novelists, then, saw in the clash between tradition and modernity an opportunity for heroism -- a particularly painful and modern form of heroism, to be sure -- Agnon sees, in the case of Yitshak Kummer at least, only victimhood. The historical vision embodied in Only Yesterday does not pit the individual against history in a struggle in which the individual's spiritual triumph is predicated upon his physical defeat or annihilation. Rather, the individual is viewed as the plaything of historical forces, the victim of objective and inevitable processes -- even though they may take the form of chance and coincidence -- that sweep man before them and then, when he least expects it, crush him.

Yitshak's role in the articulation of this historical theme helps explain the gaps which we noted earlier in the presentation of his "personality," as well as the narrator's reluctance to reveal or ponder Yitshak's inner life. One could, to be sure, ignore the narrator's advice and describe Yitshak's malady in properly clinical terms. But such analysis would not only distract us from the novel's historical theme, it would undermine it altogether. Rather than a victim of historical forces, Yitshak would become a victim of his own limitations and eccentricities, a victim, in short, of a psychological disfunction. Only Yesterday, however, is not a psychological study of the mediocrity, passivity, or vulnerability of its protagonist, but, rather, a study of the terrible impact that historical and cultural upheaval can have upon the mediocre, the passive, and the vulnerable. Yitshak is the kind of character he is because the historical vision at the heart of the novel demands such a protagonist. His actions determined by circumstance and chance, his consciousness a kind of empty vessel in which experience is dissipated in intellectual and spiritual lethargy, Yitshak's ultimate fate is neither a tragic affirmation of the human spirit nor a revelation of its psychological fragility. It is, rather, a confluence of extrapersonal forces that could no longer be avoided.

* * *

If Yitshak does his best to avoid confronting the forces that ultimately seal his fate, Balak, Only Yesterday's canine protagonist, actively seeks just such a confrontation and devotes all his canine energies to the task. For as a result of Yitshak's absent-minded prank, Balak suddenly finds himself a feared and hated outcast. Taking the words Yitshak had painted on his coat at face value, the people of Meah Shearim flee from him in terror. Later, chased and stoned wherever he turns, Balak is forced to flee for his life and wander among the gentiles of the Old City who cannot read the Hebrew words that have sealed his fate among the Jews. Distressing as his sudden exile is, however, it is the apparent gratuitousness of that exile that really torments Balak. It eventually dawns upon him that his encounter with the house painter contributed to his present circumstances, but the significance of the words painted on his back continues to evade him:

Come and see [he complains at one point]: Everyone who sees me knows the
truth about me, while I, the bearer of that truth, remain ignorant. (291)

In the end, Yitshak's unwitting prophecy is fulfilled. Tormented by a life of exile, weakened by the harsh drought that has settled over Jerusalem, and obsessed with his search for the "truth," Balak goes mad. When he finally returns to Meah Shearim, it is to seek out the author of his fate, under the delusion that he can make the truth flow out of Yitshak just as the Great Dog of canine tradition brought forth rain from the firmament by piercing it with his teeth.

Now the meaning of this intrusion of a fabulistic narrative into an otherwise realistic novel has been the focus of much critical discussion. Some critics, relying upon various psychological models, have regarded Balak as a symbolic key to the opaque personality of Yitshak Kummer. Thus, noting that dogs often appear in the novel in contexts involving women and sex, Baruch Kurzweil concludes that Balak symbolizes Yitshak's erotic drives. Reconstructing Yitshak's personality along vaguely Freudian lines, Kurzweil argues that it is Yitshak's abandonment of the restraints of traditional Jewish society, and in particular the sexual restraints, that lies at the heart of his problems. Yitshak's encounters with Balak, according to this scheme, are a symbolic externalization of Yitshak's inner struggle with a liberated Eros.[4] Turning to Jung for aid, Baruch Hochman sees Balak as a kind of alter-ego, "externalizing Yitshak's instincts in the no-man's land outside the limits of Yitshak's conscious life." Thus, according to

Hochman, whan Balak finally attacks Yitshak, the latter is in fact "succumbing to his own rage and terror."[5] Meshulam Tokhner, too, regards Yitshak and Balak as two sides of a split personality, but setting out from different premises he comes to very different conclusions. For Tokhner, the struggle between Yitshak and Balak symbolizes the conflict of the modern Jew between an irretrievable past and an uncertain future. Whereas Yitshak represents the unconscious, emotional, and "atavistic" desire to return to the past, Balak, who prevents this return, represents the "doubt-ridden consciousness" of the modern Jew. Thus, rather than symbolizing the unconscious or instinctual elements of Yitshak's personality, Balak, according to Tokhner, "embodies the crisis of Judaism."[6]

Treating Yitshak and Balak as two elements or emanations of one personality does seem to solve several apparent difficulties. For one thing, it justifies Agnon's deviation from the realistic norms he establishes in the first half of the novel. Through the fable, the unconscious roots of Yitshak's malaise, only hinted at in the realistic sphere of the novel, are made explicit. Or, if we follow Tokhner's interpretation, the specific historical factors that determine Yitshak's fate are, through the fable, given precise, allegorical expression. In either case, the final, fatal encounter between man and dog at the end of the novel is provided with a clear symbolic justification. It represents, depending upon whose view you accept, the triumph of repressed drives that had been seething all along beneath the placid narrative surface, or the "end of the illusion of reconciliation" between the past and present.

There are, however, crucial limitations in attempting to fuse Yitshak and Balak into one composite personality. Balak, after all, has a distinct life of his own, and Agnon develops his character and fate with at least as much care as he does that of his human protagonist. Thus, to reduce Balak to a simple externalization of unconscious drives violates our sense of his vitality and integrity as a fictional personage. In spite of his canine habits, Balak suffers real anguish, and is able to express that anguish far more articulately than his human counterpart. As Tokhner correctly observes, it is Balak who is the "dialectician" while Yitshak typically caves in to vague emotions and impulse. As a result, Balak is in many ways a more appealing character than Yitshak, and one can indeed argue, as does Eli Shvaid, that he emerges as the real hero of the novel.[7]

What is perhaps most disturbing about these attempts to interpret the Balak fable, however, is the need the critics apparently feel to render it intelligible by reducing it to a simple allegory, to come up with -- in spite of the narrator's own protests and warnings -- an unequivocal and definitive "meaning." It is as if they view the fable's ambiguities as mere obstacles which it is the critic's duty to circumnavigate at all costs. The psycho-theological interpretation of Yitshak's character that Kurzweil derives from the Balak fable will come as no surprise to readers familiar with Kurzweil's work. He discovers a similar "meaning" at the heart of nearly all the works of modern Hebrew literature he analyzes. Tokhner makes no effort to disguise his allegorical intent, as the title of his book, Cipher to Agnon, makes clear. In true allegorical fashion, Tohkner's "deciphering" of the Balak fable reduces it to an unambiguous and rather commonplace historical schema. In spite of the enigmatic qualities that Agnon gives to the fable, it is not totally indeterminate or meaningless. But in addition to the fact that these allegorical interpretations ignore the positive functions that ambiguity may fulfill, they aim for a degree of specificity that needlessly closes off the horizon of meaning which is the very source of the fable's power.

However, to insist upon Balak's status in the novel as a character in his own right, or upon the enigmatic qualities of his fable, is not to deny the obvious parallels that exist between man and dog in Only Yesterday. On the contrary, it is precisely through an examination of these parallels, and the variety of ways in which Agnon pursues them, that we can begin to clarify the relationship between the novel's two protagonists and, ultimately, the role that Balak and his fable play in the overall structure of the novel. As Gershon Shaked has amply demonstrated in his study of Agnon's shorter fiction, the technique of narrative parallelism and analogy is central to Agnon's art.[8] Typically, Agnon develops a series of apparently random, loosely linked sub-plots which, upon closer inspection, represent subtle but meaningful variations upon one narrative or thematic structure. Now, the parallels between the fates of Yitshak Kummer and Balak are clear enough. Both are uprooted from their homes by forces beyond their understanding and control. Both seek to put an end to their uprootedness by returning to the world from which they had been exiled. And for both, the attempt to return ends in madness and death.

Having set up these outward parallels between Yitshak's story and the Balak fable, however, Agnon spares no effort in obscuring the "deeper" connections between the stories. One way he does this is by periodically stressing the artificiality of the fable and flaunting the gap between the tale and its meaning. Thus, within the fable itself Agnon includes a satirical account of the efforts of the "opinion makers" of Jaffa to come up with its true meaning:

> One would say there is a hidden meaning here; another would say that the hidden meaning must be inferred from the plain meaning. Yet no one could agree on what the plain meaning was. Meanwhile, opinions proliferated until there were as many opinions as there were people in the city of Jaffa. (459)

By "baring the device" in this way, Agnon places the reader (and the literary "opinion maker") in a difficult situation. Having thrown into question the very legitimacy of allegorical interpretation, the novelist can evoke possibilities of meaning even as he subverts our efforts to pin it down.

"The historian," Agnon's non-commital narrator comments at one point, "will have to labor a great deal before he will discover where men's affairs end and the affairs of dogs begin." (470) This deliberate obscuring of the border between the human and animal realms is the source of much of the enigmatic quality of Agnon's fable. For Balak's story does not simply represent an inferior, degraded, or "bestialized" version of the human drama. Balak is, to be sure, emphatically canine. "Balak," the narrator tells us, "was a simple dog and did not concern himself with matters that exceed the bounds of common sense." (468) Even as he suffers the pangs of exile, Balak pursues the habitual pleasures of his species. He sniffs, he scratches, he relieves himself in suitable nooks and crannies.

His immediate concerns are to find a comfortable hole in which to curl up for the night, a bone to gnaw upon, a chance to snarl at one of his enemies. But in some ways Balak is more "human" than his human counterpart and, indeed, displays many of the heroic qualities of the talush as he was often portrayed in earlier Hebrew novels. Balak is far more articulate and assertive than Yitshak, far more typical of the talush in his critical self-consciousness and intellectual honesty. Unlike Yitshak, Balak insists upon confronting his fate and uses all of his canine powers to discover the reason behind his exile. Rather than ignoring or evading fundamental issues, he pursues them relentlessly and, as a result, he goes mad.

The manner in which Agnon insists upon Balak's superior intellectual and spiritual qualities, on the one hand, and his earthy canine disposition, on the other, has much in common with Kafka's manipulation of the fable form in which "less-than-human beings... inevitably turn out to possess more-than-human qualities."[9] Thus, in the course of presenting a dispassionate and absolutely lucid account of his former life as an ape, the speaker in Kafka's "A Report to an Academy," can point out in passing that the "fine, clear train of thought" which led to his decision to become human, "... must have [been] constructed somehow within my belly, since apes think with their bellies."[10] Similarly, Kafka's dog in "Investigations of a Dog" who, like Balak, becomes obsessed with his search for the truth ("For all the senseless phenomena of our existence, and the most senseless by far of all, are susceptible of investigation."[11]) has to begin with what, for a dog, is the "essence of all knowledge," the injunction, "Water the ground as much as you can."[12] For Kafka, as for Agnon, the animal-speakers of their fables are both less-than-human and more-than-human, seekers of clarity and truth yet condemned to pursue their investigations from within their animal perspective and sensibility.

While such a situation can be a source of pathos, Agnon, again like Kafka, exploits the comic potential of his fable-creature's distinctly canine sensibility to great effect. Balak's investigations into the truth about his fate, for example, are mixed with learned digressions on various aspects of canine lore, a branch of learning that includes history, legend, myth, as well as science and psychology. Balak draws inspiration from one of his illustrious ancestors (just as Yitshak draws inspiration from his ancestor, Reb Yudel Hasid) who, according to canine tradition, at one time ruled over a large part of Jerusalem. It was a dog, according to Balak and canine cosmology, who was responsible for the creation of the rains, as well as the moon and the stars. "That is why," the narrator remarks, "dogs bark at the moon; they are recalling the great labor of their ancestor, the Great Dog..." (474). From his knowledge of dogs and his observation of men, Balak finds ample evidence for the widespread canine belief that dogs were originally men who, having rebelled against the Creator, were condemned to their present status. About this belief, the narrator offers the following equivocation:

> We do not know if Balak held this opinion as a result of extreme naivete or whether it was based upon observation, since he had seen many human beings with canine dispositions. (472)

The canine comedy that Agnon erects around Balak's fable balances precariously upon the calculated ambiguity of this remark. Threading its way through the last rather somber chapters of the novel, the Balak fable offers welcome comic relief from the lugubrious course of Yitshak's gradual decline. Yet the narrator's constant if muted suggestions of a more serious connection between man and dog forces us to wonder whether it is simply Balak's canine sensibility that is responsible for his opinions, or whether there is something more to the apparent foolishness. Are we in the end supposed to take Balak seriously and, if so, how seriously?

By reducing the human drama of <u>Only Yesterday</u> to canine proportions and constantly playing upon the comic "bisociation" of the human and animal realms that is made possible by the fable form, Agnon effectively parodies Yitshak Kummer's struggle and, indeed, the entire <u>talush</u> tradition.[13] As the Russian Formalists recognized, however, the essence of parody lies not only in its comic rejection of old forms, but in its ability to find new possibilities of expression in them. As Victor Erlich describes it, "the old is presented, as it were, in a new key. The obsolete device is not thrown overboard, but repeated in a new incongruous context and thus either rendered absurd... or made 'perceptible' again."[14] The new context in this case is the canine world and sensibility of Balak and while the incongruity of this context casts an absurd light upon the human drama, the humor of the parody is darkened by the paradoxical fact that the canine perspective, in spite of its "extreme naivete," or perhaps precisely because of it, turns out to be far superior to the human perspective. As a result, even as we smile at Balak's limitations, we also come to sympathize with him. If Yitshak's passivity and mute acceptance are difficult to understand, we have no difficulty understanding why Balak insists upon discovering the source of his own exile:

Why am I cast out of the whole world? Why does everyone seek my life? Have I done anyone harm? Have I bitten anyone? Then why do they pursue me so that my bones have no rest? Balak directed his complaint to heaven and howled, <u>hav</u>, <u>hav</u>, let me have a place to rest, let me have justice! (475)

Balak, for all his limitations and canine quirks, understands precisely what is at stake in the fate he shares with his human counterpart and can articulate both his understanding and his protest in a manner that would be unthinkable from Yitshak Kummer. "It is great art in my view," the narrator-hero of Agnon's earlier novel, <u>A Guest for the Night</u>, says at one point, "when one speaks of happy things with a sad voice and of sad things in a happy voice." Following the advice of the Guest, Agnon explores the most sinister aspects of Yitshak Kummer's fate in a fable that is also a comic <u>tour de force</u>.

But the fable does more than provide a "happy voice" in which to make explicit the very sad point of Yitshak's story. The fable form is by its very nature an abstracting medium, encouraging us to look beyond the specific instance to the more general and universal. Thus, while Yitshak's fate is firmly embedded in the social geography of the Second Aliyah, the Balak fable wrenches that fate from its historical matrix and, as a result, gives it unmistakable metaphysical overtones. If Yitshak, in his role as <u>talush</u>, represents a generation victimized by overwhelming circumstances, Balak emerges as an archetypal figure whose fate encompasses but finally transcends temporal and spatial boundaries. For Balak, history is not the culprit but rather the human (or, in his case, the canine) condition.

Let us compare, by way of illustration, the role that insanity plays in the talush tradition with Agnon's treatment of Balak's decline into madness. Nahman, the protagonist of Fierberg's Whither?, is torn between his loyalty to the Jewish world of his upbringing and the promise of spiritual freedom and growth that seems to exist only beyond the narrow confines of tradition. Unable to understand Nahman's struggle, the local Jewish community attributes his erratic behavior to mental deficiency, and he is soon referred to as Nahman the meshuga. While the epithet is clearly exaggerated, Nahman does indeed become a reclusive malcontent, rocked by alternating bouts of despair and fantastic visions of Jewish revival in the Near East. Feuermann, the protagonist of Brenner's In Winter, similarly despairs over his inability to sever the bonds that tie him to his Jewish past, and his efforts in this direction lead him to the verge of madness and suicide. And madness is indeed the fate of Ya'akov Abramoson, the protagonist of Brenner's second novel, Beside the Point. Abramoson is divided between his loyalty to Hebrew literature as a means to Jewish national revival and the more fashionable "universalistic" ideals urged upon him by Hava, the object of his erotic longings. Just as he seems ready to abandon his Jewish preoccupations, news of violent pogroms in several Jewish communities reaches him. This new development is too much for him and, once more caught between conflicting loyalties, he suffers a nervous breakdown. In the talush literature, then, madness is essentially a social malady whose origins are firmly rooted in the circumstances of Jewish life in the modern world. It is the fate of men who, searching for a new, liberated existence, abandon the moribund precincts of their native ground and, as a result, find themselves caught between two worlds, neither of which they can call home. The talush is a victim of an age of transition and crisis; in better times and circumstances he might have maintained his balance.

Balak, like the conventional talush, and like Yitshak, is uprooted from his native ground. His madness, however, is not so much a result of external circumstances as it is the outcome of his desire to discover the "truth" behind those circumstances. There must be, Balak insists, a reasonable explanation of his sudden exile, and he spares no efforts to discover it. As the narrator explains:

> There is a covenant with the truth so that whoever seeks it, seeks all of it. Such was Balak. Since he had put his mind to the truth, he was not satisfied with a part of it, but wanted to know the whole truth. (292)

Ironically, Balak discovers the truth about his exile early in his quest, but he dismisses it as too unreasonable:

> Balak wagged his tail and said, it's just as I suspected. I have only others to blame for my troubles. It is on account of that n'er-do-well who put some marks on my back. But do I deserve to be pursued just because some n'er-do-well wrote some words on my back? (292)

Balak will only be content with a reasonable explanation for his fate; to ascribe it to a thoughtless prank boggles even the canine imagination.

Balak's attempts to discover the "whole truth" always end in frustration. Wherever he turns he sees clear and invariably painful evidence of his new status as exile, but nowhere can he find an explanation for it. Nevertheless, he refuses to give up and his quest for the truth quickly becomes an all-consuming obsession. At times delirious, at other times too lucid for his own good, Balak's thought processes lapse into a kind of runaway cerebration in which sense and nonsense contend with each other.

> Balak gathered up his legs, closed his eyes and, lying there, reflected upon the same things over which thinkers of all generations have labored. What are we? What is our life? Are all the pains and torments and troubles that afflict us worth the little, ephemeral comforts we seek? Especially for the likes of me, one who lacks even the simplest comfort, who knows only endless labors, each one more exhausting than the last. (575)

Balak, for the moment, sees clearly into his fate and can reflect upon it in the same terms that "thinkers of all generations" have reflected upon similar fates. In the face of unexplained suffering and the inevitable torments and afflictions that are the fate of all living beings, what, Balak asks, is the purpose of our lives and our strivings for comfort and pleasure? It is just such moments of lucidity, however, that push Balak to the edge of madness. Thus, immediately following these reflections, as Balak begins to take note of his deteriorating mental condition, his thought dissolves into a hodge-podge of bits of scholastic science, philosophy, psychology, folklore and superstition:

> Balak... was not inclined to the opinion of philosophers who contend that madness comes from black bile rather than from evil spirits. He accepted only a part of their claim; black bile is the immediate cause, but it, in turn, is caused by evil spirits... And there can be no doubt that the evil spirits who haunted the wind-mill created the black bile... since, as is well known, nothing in nature suffers a vacuum. Since the wind-mill had been deserted by men, the evil spirits had made it their home. (575-576)

This jumble of scholastic sense and superstitious nonsense distracts Balak, and the reader, from the somber implications of his earlier reflections. The question of unexplained suffering seems to get lost in the shuffle, and the spiritual origin of Balak's madness is reduced to questions of black bile, evil spirits, and vacuums. The distraction, however, is only temporary. Balak does not give up his search for the truth, and, in the end, he returns to Meah Shearim to find it, even though he knows such a return means certain death.

Madness, then, is the price Balak pays for struggling to make sense out of an absurd fate, for contending with forces he cannot identify, much less confront. In this sense, he has more in common with Joseph K. than with Kafka's animal-protagonists. For someone has apparently traduced Balak, and he is condemned to a futile search for the source and substance of the claim held against him. And like Kafka's protagonist, the more Balak searches for this "truth," the more distant and elusive it seems to be. Now in <u>The Trial</u>, we never learn precisely what it is that Joseph K. is guilty of; like the accused man himself, the reader can only speculate as to the nature of the omnipresent but elusive court's proceedings.[15] In the case of Balak, however, the reader knows at the outset that no crime has been committed and that Balak's "punishment" is as absurd and meaningless as it appears to its victim. When he demands justice from the silent heavens, then, Balak's "naivete" sounds anything but canine.

Balak finds neither justice nor truth, but, upon his return to Meah Shearim, he does find Yitshak Kummer. Noting that of all the inhabitants of the quarter only Yitshak shows no fear of him and recalling their earlier encounter, Balak becomes convinced that Yitshak possesses the truth he desperately seeks. Rocked by despair and rage, Balak attacks Yitshak, believing that the truth will flow from Yitshak's wounds just as the "blessed rains" fell from the sky when the Great Dog pierced the firmament. This last confrontation between Yitshak and Balak marks the final convergence of the realistic and fabulistic spheres of Only Yesterday. Balak, the "allegorical" dog, becomes a flesh and blood presence and, intruding himself into the realistic course of events, brings it to a sudden, if not totally unexpected, conclusion. The effect of this narrative sleight of hand is to confirm our suspicions that the "truth" which Balak had been pursuing is the same "truth" that Yitshak, until now, has successfully evaded. In their first encounter, Yitshak had condemned Balak to a life of exile and alienation by labeling him a mad dog. Now, Yitshak's unwitting prophecy having been fulfilled, Balak's infectious bite undoes Yitshak's efforts to end his own "exile" by establishing himself in Meah Shearim. Man and dog are destined to share the same fate. Indeed, rumors later circulate in Meah Shearim that toward the end of his ordeal Yitshak crawled about on all fours and howled like a mad dog.

If Yitshak's story suggests the powerlessness of the individual before the crushing circumstances of history, Balak's fate suggests the futility of man's efforts to elicit meaning from those circumstances, to discover the "truth" that lies behind them. Whether one evades the "truth" or attempts to confront it, man remains the plaything of forces beyond his control and understanding. Insofar as we are all victims of an impenetrable fate, the fable suggests, we are all uprooted men. And insofar as we insist upon discovering the "truth" about that fate, our naive and futile efforts take on a ridiculous canine quality. If, as Reb Gronam Yekum Purkan asserts, "the face of the generation is the face of a dog," it is the face of a generation engaged in a futile and ultimately farcical quest for a "truth" that is as absurd as it seems.

* * *

With its human and canine protagonists, Only Yesterday provides us with a unique opportunity to observe the manner in which the protagonist's participation in the narrative structure and the function which he serves in that structure influence and at times dictate the kind of "character" he shall be as well as the manner in which the author reveals that "character." Yitshak, as we have seen, must be a mediocre, drab, and listless character if he is to fulfill the function Agnon sets for him in his chronicle of the Second Aliyah. By passively responding from a position of innocence and naivete to the historical, social and cultural forces that confront him, Yitshak reflects the terrible power of those forces, their capacity to overwhelm and ultimately destroy the individual who, consciously or unconsciously, attempts to avoid them. Moreover, able to move easily from milieu to milieu by virtue of his mediocrity and purposelessness, Yitshak enables Agnon to explore both the allurements and limitations of various responses to history.

Yitshak is the kind of character he is because the overall conceptions of Only Yesterday requires such a character. But that conception does not require, as in the case of Abramovitsh's The Beggars' Book, a total rejection of psychological coherence or verisimilitude. Yitshak's passivity, his refusal or inability to come to grips with his circumstances, may at times give cause to wonder, but we are provided with enough information -- explicit narrative commentary, narrated and quoted monologue, speculation, hints, symbolic patterns -- at least to imagine the psychological sources of his listlessness. Indeed, it is precisely the reticence of Agnon's narrator to fathom the depths of Yitshak's psyche -- his resort to selective omniscience, his equivocations and obfuscations -- that leave us room for such imaginings.

Agnon's introduction of a canine protagonist into the realistic framework of Only Yesterday, on the other hand, provides us with perhaps the clearest possible example of a case where the requirements of the narrative dictate the nature of the protagonist. There can be no more radical deviation from the norms of realism and psychological verisimilitude than a fable in which human concerns, thoughts, and emotions are placed in the mind and mouth of an animal. Agnon uses this "deviation" both to parody Yitshak's ordeal and the talush tradition as a whole and, at the same time, explore the most sinister and threatening aspects of his vision of the human condition. The constant juxtaposition of canine comedy and existential despair which the fable and its protagonist make possible is designed to sabotage the reader's stereotypical emotional response and forestall reactions of empathy and pity which a writer like Brenner is intent upon provoking. By forcing us to smile even as he confronts us with the ultimate absurdity of meaningless annihilation, Agnon deflects but never denies the immediate impact of his novel's nihilistic burden.

CHAPTER SEVEN

Conclusion

The functional roles played by the protagonists we have considered in this study as well as the techniques devoted to their construction vary greatly. Given this variety, it seems clear that no single model of narrative, particularly one based upon observation of the "systematic correlation of terms denoting action," can provide an adequate basis for a poetics of fictional character. For to reduce Mendele, Yermiah Feuermann, Yehezkel Hefetz, Yitshak Kummer, or Balak to an "agent of action," one would have to ignore so much that the resulting taxonomy could hardly do justice to the character or to the narrative structure in which he participates. Most importantly, that which would be ignored in such an analysis -- specific attributes, psychological motivation, modes and techniques of character construction -- may be, as I have attempted to demonstrate, absolutely necessary for the proper realization of other elements of the narrative structure, not the least among them, the plot.

Nor is it sufficient simply to observe the quantity of narrative units denoting a character's attributes and, on that basis, to divide narrative into two or three broad categories or tendencies. This is, essentially, what Roland Barthes does in his "Introduction to the Structural Analysis of Narratives" when he proposes a classification of narratives according to the preponderance of "functions" or "indices." Thus, according to Barthes, psychological narratives are "heavily indicial," while narratives that fall between psychological fiction and "heavily functional" folktales are to be considered "intermediary forms."[1] But as Todorov recognized, it is not merely the quantity of attributional propositions that determines whether a given narrative is psychological, but rather the nature of the relationship between such propositions and propositions of action and, ultimately, whether actions, as expressions of character, contribute to a psychologically coherent system.[2]

But even Todorov's distinction does not go far enough. For, still operating under the assumption that actions and events constitute the basic units of narrative, Todorov insists that, even in psychological narrative, psychological causality merely "duplicates" the causality of events. Thus, even if we can derive a psychologically coherent system from the actions of characters, this system is only a "by-product" that exists on "another level" from that of actions. Such a hierarchical formulation -- indeed, the very terminology employed -- harks back to the Russian Formalists' distinction between bound and free motifs, and thus leaves little room for an analysis of the interaction, not to mention the shifting of hierarchies, that can occur between attributes and action, character and plot.

In spite of the general failure of the narratologists to find a place for characters and their attributes in their typologies and taxonomies, they do provide us with some principles that might serve as the basis for a poetics of character in narrative discourse. Among those principles, we might include the following: (1) narrative personages are more profitably analyzed as constructs than as real people, (2) the principle of construction of narrative personages is not exclusively or necessarily based upon considerations of mimesis but rather, (3) the fictional personage's function in the narrative structure in which he participates dictates -- to one degree or another -- both his character and the techniques through which that character is revealed. On the other hand, the notion that the character of fictional personages is dictated exclusively by their function in the narrative structure, especially when that function is construed in terms of actions necessary for the coherence of the plot, is neither accurate nor very useful. The character of fictional personages results from the interaction between the requirements of narrative structure and the requirements of mimesis derived from a particular but by no means universal ideology of character that will vary according to historical and generic factors. The proper aim of structural analysis, it seems to me, is to expose and clarify the nature of that interaction.

The first step in such an analysis is to determine the character of the fictional personage by identifying and linking up the narrative units expressive of character (both explicit and implicit, homogeneous and heterogeneous) scattered along the text continuum. This is, of course, a rather traditional approach except that, traditionally, character analysis usually stops at this point. Our next step would be to examine the relationship between the character pattern that has emerged, the ideology of character it suggests, and the kinds of units (narrator's description or commentary, action, dialogue, narrated monologue, etc.) that make up the pattern, on the one hand, and other patterns within the overall narrative structure, i.e., plot, setting, theme, symbolic configuration, etc., on the other hand.

Now, in any given text, and even within a given text, this relationship can vary greatly. Let me suggest, however, three categories of relationship that may serve as useful points of reference. First, the character pattern may form a coherent system in terms of one or another ideology of character (folk wisdom, social or historical determinism, psychology, etc.) which is, nevertheless, largely independent of or irrelevant to other patterns in the narrative structure, as, for example, in many folktales and their derivatives. Second, the character pattern may be more or less congruent with other patterns within the narrative structure. That is, the character's actions, attributes, thoughts, beliefs, etc., form a coherent pattern among themselves, but at the same time these elements of character serve essential functions in other patterns. This relationship of congruence, as Barthes argues, is by its nature undecidable and, moreover, a distinguishing mark of classically realistic fiction. While it is true that Barthes at times attempts to decide the undecidable, Hrushovski reminds us that the subordination of one pattern to another is characteristically a temporary matter, dependent upon the local needs of the narrative or the interests of the reader.

Finally, the character pattern may be consistently or intermittently in a relationship of tension or dissonance with other patterns within the narrative structure. This dissonance, however, can work in two directions. First, the requirements of the ideology of character operative in the text can lead to the distortion or subversion of other patterns. Thus, in narratives in which characters are constructed according to classically realistic norms, these characters, as Forster puts it, are "often engaged in treason against the main scheme of the book." Put in our terms, the "realistic" presentation of character may result in a weak plot or an unclear or contradictory thematic pattern. Conversely, the requirements of plot or theme may lead to distortion or subversion of the character pattern. The result would be a "flat" character or the kind of "illegal" character which Barthes refers to as a figure.

These three categories of relationship -- independence, congruence, dissonance -- when used as points of reference rather than as the basis for a static typology, can help us determine the structural role or function of characters in a wide variety of texts. The analysis of individual texts should, of course, reveal significant variations and nuances. Let us attempt, then, to place the novels we have considered in the schema I have proposed.

In the case of Abramovitsh's The Beggars' Book, we found that a sustained analysis of the narrator-hero, Mendele, yielded a highly contradictory character. His identity constantly oscillating between "everyday Jew" and distanced, ironic, often cynical observer of Jewish society, Mendele seemed like a quick-change artist capable of metamorphosing before our very eyes. As we noted, critics intent upon naturalizing this state of affairs expended great energy and considerable ingenuity in providing biographical, sociological, and philosophical explanations for Mendele's multiple identities. Our method, on the other hand, led us to accept the fact that Mendele does not cohere, and to search for the origin of this subversion of realistic norms of characterization in Mendele's function in the narrative structure in which he participates. As a result, we discovered that Mendele's tendency to "break up into little pieces" is dictated by Abramovitsh's thematic objectives, in particular his need to defamiliarize Jewish society in order to generate a more complex view of it. Thus, in terms of the schema I have proposed, The Beggars' Book provides us with a clear-cut example of dissonance. The "character" of the protagonist is undermined and ultimately subverted by the requirements of the narrative.

At first glance, Brenner's novels seem to present us with dissonance in the other direction. For, as we have seen, the character of the protagonists constitutes the narratives' regulating principle, dictating both style and structure. Critics pursuing traditional methods of analysis have argued that, as a result, both the style and the structure of Brenner's novels seem needlessly flawed. But when analyzed in reference to the character of the protagonists, these flaws prove to be not flaws at all, but integral elements of the character pattern and thus of the overall narrative structure which is consistently subordinated to this pattern. Thus, what seems like dissonance is in fact an example of congruence of the highest order. "Yes, my past is gloomy, wretched, and vulgar [Yermiah Feuermann states at one point] because it is mine, the past of a man like me; and yet, to considerable extent, I am what I am because I have a past like that, a past of littleness, a gloomy, wretched, vulgar past."[3] Feuermann's inability to decide whether his past is a function of his character or his character a function of his past aptly expresses the undecidability of the congruent text.

In Brenner's novels, every action, whether it is the object of narration or the act of narration itself, serves, ultimately, as an index of character. And every explicit notation of character, whether presented in the voice of the narrator or that of the protagonist himself, contributes to other patterns in the narrative structure and, ultimately, renders them intelligible. Brenner's novels clearly show the deficiency of analyses -- whether traditional or structural -- which, for the sake of rigor, isolate one pattern rather than viewing it in terms of its interaction, and interdependence, with the manifold patterns of which narrative structures are composed.

Agnon's *Only Yesterday* presents us with another kind of congruent text, one that is more closely aligned with the classically realistic text. Nevertheless, it is not free of dissonance, most obviously in the introduction of Balak, but also in the characterization of Yitshak Kummer. As we have seen, some critics have attempted to provide insight into Yitshak's rather opaque personality through a kind of psychological allegorization of Balak's fable, in spite of the narrator's own equivocations and obfuscations on this point. It was my argument, on the other hand, that this narrative reticence and the general sketchiness of Yitshak's psychological portrait (a form of dissonance in the context of a realistic novel) are not to be ignored or explained away, but rather to be considered in relation to the overall structure and conception of the novel. Thus, I argued that Yitshak's docile behavior, his lethargic thought processes, and the narrator's refusal to provide a definitive, unambiguous explanation for them serve the needs of a chronicle-like narrative in which historical and social forces, not human personality, are the prime movers. At the same time, however, the narrator's reticence does not deny Yitshak a psychological essence; it merely, as it were, pushes it into the narrative background.

With Balak, on the other hand, Agnon completely rejects the mimetic imperatives of the congruent narrative. Or, rather, he exploits the opportunity afforded by the fable to play the demands of mimesis against those of literary convention to great effect, both "enigmatic" and comic. Moreover, the Balak fable does indeed shift the novel's frame of reference, not from history to psychology, as argued by Kurzweil and Hochman, but from history to the human condition. Through Balak -- part dog, part man, part symbol -- Agnon exposes the nihilistic conclusions of the novel which ultimately reduce history to a specific instance of man's absurd struggle to discover a truth that is not there, or at least that is not accessible to man or dog. And only Balak -- certainly not Yitshak -- could reveal that absurdity and at the same time invest the struggle with a paradoxical sense of grandeur and elevation.

What, finally, can our analyses of the protagonists of four Hebrew novels contribute to the literary history of modern Hebrew literature? Until relatively recently, historians of modern Hebrew literature have been preoccupied with the elucidation of "great themes" (usually as indices of extraliterary historical or social phenomena) or the analysis of protagonists as "representatives" of this or that generation. There is, to be sure, some justification for this approach. The roughly three-quarters of a century in which the four novels we have considered were written was a period of radical change in the internal and external conditions of Jewish life. The process of political emancipation in Western

Conclusion

Europe was, by the beginning of this period, already subject to the pressures of anti-semitic protests, while in Eastern Europe Czarist oppression threatened the very physical existence of the Jews. At the same time, the secularization of Jewish life promoted by assimilation in the West and "enlightenment" in the East undermined the traditional Jewish community from within. By the end of the period, six million Jews had perished at the hands of the Nazis, over three million Jews had emigrated to the United States, and a much smaller group, emboldened with dreams of national revival, settled in Palestine where they eventually established an independent Jewish state. These massive physical and cultural dislocations were accompanied by great spiritual and ideological turmoil as Jews attempted to make sense of, or merely to cope with, their belated entry into modernity. In such circumstances, the temptation to interpret works of imaginative literature in terms of history, as both the reflections of major events and trends and as keys to their understanding, can be quite compelling.

But all forms of representation, including historical and scientific discourse, are mediated, subject to systems of control, principles of constraint, rules of exclusion, limitation, and appropriation.[4] Imaginative literature, in this respect, is only the most overtly and self-consciously mediated form of representation. Literary conventions, generic expectations and norms, and principles of internal coherence, even as they reflect issues in society, have an inner dynamic of their own and thus constitute a proper sphere of independent study. More importantly, however, the analysis of the forms of mediation operative in works of imaginative literature can reveal the underlying principles that shape and ultimately determine the representation of reality.

From this perspective, then, it is less important to argue whether Abramovitsh's representation of Jewish life in the Pale provides us with a "genuinely realistic description" (Tsemah, Rabinovich), or whether the content of his satirical critique is fair-minded, morally justified, or politically desirable (Kariv), than it is to note that Abramovitsh represents the individual as a social creature whose behavior is entirely determined from without and that, as a result, a "realistic" analysis of his protagonist stumbles upon contradictions and discontinuities that resist the superimposition of a semiotics of psychology. Similarly, it is less important to determine whether the pronouncements of Brenner's protagonists on the Jewish predicament, on the future of the Jewish people, on Socialism, Zionism, and a host of other "public" issues are historically accurate or internally coherent (Kurzweil) than to note that Brenner represents the individual as a psychological creature whose response to both public issues and private concerns is determined, largely, by inner conflicts in a constant state of development. Brenner's radical subjectivism, his subordination of all narrative elements (including, in the first-person narratives, the act of narration itself) to the revelation of the "atmosphere of the mind," requires that we reassess the traditional distinction between plot, character, and setting and, moreover, the very nature of the "truth" that fiction purports to tell or reflect. Finally, it is less important to posit a psycho-theological basis for the listlessness and ultimate fate of Agnon's protagonist (Kurzweil, Hochman), or to "decipher" Agnon's enigmatic allegories in order to reduce them to an unambiguous -- and rather commonplace -- historical schema (Tokhner), than it is to note that Agnon's representation of the individual as the object of historical and existential forces he can neither identify nor control leads him to "decenter" the identity of the protagonist, to limit (selectively) the omniscience of his narrator and, finally, to adopt a mode of narrative discourse in which enigma, ambiguity, and multivalence serve important functions.

The variety of ways in which these protagonists participate in the narratives in which they appear as well as the diverse modes and techniques of characterization that we analyzed are clearly symptomatic of a more general set of discontinuities that characterize Hebrew fiction in the decades before and after the turn of the last century. Indeed, one might argue that this plethora of modes of narrative discourse is the most significant aspect of modern Hebrew literary history. Literary analysis that ignores or minimizes these differences in a quest for overarching historical themes must necessarily distort both the individual works and the history.

NOTES TO CHAPTER ONE

1. See David Patterson, Abraham Mapu: The Creator of the Modern Hebrew Novel (London, 1964), pp. 63-85; on the "compulsive didacticism" and "pathetically restricted linguistic resources" of the novelists who followed Mapu, see his The Hebrew Novel in Czarist Russia (Edinburgh, 1964).

2. Gershon Shaked, Hasiporet ha'ivrit: 1880-1970 [Hebrew Narrative Fiction 1880-1970] (Jerusalem, 1978), I, 32.

3. On the circumstances of Hebrew literature at the turn of the century see Dov Sadan, Avnei bedek [Touchstones] (Tel Aviv, 1962), pp. 9-68; Shaked, Hasiporet ha'ivrit, pp. 19-68; Dan Miron, "Hebrew Literature at the Beginning of the Twentieth Century" [Hebrew], Me'asef agudat hasofrim, 2 (1961), 436-464; Robert Alter, "Hebrew Literature and the Paradox of Survival," in After the Tradition: Essays on Modern Jewish Writing (New York, 1971), pp. 79-94; Avraham Sha'anan, Hasifrut ha'ivrit hahadasha lizerameha [Trends in Modern Hebrew Literature], II, III, IV (Tel Aviv, 1962-1967).

4. M.Z. Feierberg, Whither? and Other Stories, trans. Hillel Halkin (Philadelphia, 1973), p. 205.

5. A summary of the lecture was published in the November 10th issue of the Hebrew weekly Hayehudi. See Yitshak Bakon, Brenner hatsa'ir [The Young Brenner] (Tel Aviv, 1975), I, 147.

6. Kol kitvei Y.H. Brenner [The Complete Writings of Y.H. Brenner], III (Tel Aviv, 1967), 63; see also Shemuel Werses, "Between Brenner and Mendele" [Hebrew], Mahbarot leheker yetsirato ufe'ulo shel Y.H. Brenner (Tel Aviv, 1975), pp. 31-53.

7. Kol kitvei Y.H. Brenner, II, 262; the article originally appeared in Hapo'el hatsa'ir in 1909.

8. Yitshak Bakon surveys Brenner's published criticism of Agnon's early works in "Brenner on S.Y. Agnon" [Hebrew], Me'oznaim 27:3-4 (1968), 210-216.

9. Quoted by Bakon, "Brenner on S.Y. Agnon," p. 215.

10. Arnold Band in Nostalgia and Nightmare: A Study in the Fiction of S.Y. Agnon (Berkeley, 1968) sets the date of Agnon's arrival at 1907. Yitshak Bakon argues convincingly for 1908. See his "On the Year of Agnon's Aliyah and its Implications" [Hebrew], Hapo'el hatsa'ir 39:27-28 (April 1968), 23-25.

11. S.Y. Agnon, "Yosef Haim Brenner in Life and Death" [Hebrew] in Me'atsmi le'atsmi [From Me to Myself] (Jerusalem, 1976), pp. 111-141.

12. Rafael Weiser, "S.Y. Agnon's Letters to Y.H. Brenner" [Hebrew] in S.Y. Agnon: Mekharim ute'udot [S.Y. Agnon: Studies and Documents], eds. G. Shaked and R. Weiser (Jerusalem, 1978), p. 43; on Agnon's struggle to "overcome" the influence of Brenner, see Gershon Shaked, Omanut hasipur shel S.Y. Agnon [The Narrative Art of S.Y. Agnon] (Merhavia, 1973), pp. 13-42.

13. S.Y. Agnon, "Yosef Haim Brenner in Life and Death," p. 128.

14. Ibid., p. 136.

15. S.Y. Agnon, Temol Shilshom [Only Yesterday] in Kol sipurav shel Shemuel Yosef Agnon [The Complete Stories of Shemuel Yosef Agnon], V (Jerusalem, 1968), pp. 381-382.

16. S.Y. Agnon, "Yosef Haim Brenner in Life and Death," p. 138.

17. On maskilic attitudes toward Yiddish, see Dan Miron, A Traveler Disguised: A Study of Modern Yiddish Fiction in the Nineteenth Century (New York, 1973), pp. 34-66.

18. H.N. Bialik, "The Creator of the Nusah" [Hebrew] in Kol kitvei H.N. Bialik [The Complete Writings of H.N. Bialik] (Tel Aviv, 1971), pp. 245-246; on the nature and influence of the nusah, see Shaked, Hasiporet ha'ivrit, pp. 83-89.

19. Gershon Shaked, Ben sehok ledema [Between Laughter and Tears], 2nd ed. (Ramat Gan, 1974).

20. For a "composite biography" of Brenner's generation and its relationship to the previous generation, see Miron, "Hebrew Literature at the Beginning of the Twentieth Century."

21. On Brenner's first stay in Bialystok, see Bakon, Brenner hatsa'ir, pp. 28-50.

22. Quoted in Bakon, Brenner hatsa'ir, p. 65.

23. Ibid., p. 66.

24. Amir Gilboa, the contemporary Israeli poet, recalls his childhood image of Brenner in this manner: "My first Brenner -- one of the three Titans of my childhood. The two others, A.D. Gordon and Trumpeldor. Thus they appeared to me when I first met them on the button on the lapel of my older brother's jacket, a member of Hehaluts. In one, the oldest among them, I saw the worker of the Land, the Land of my dreams; in the second, Trumpeldor, I discovered the hero who with his last breath bequeathed his famous last testament. In Brenner, meanwhile, I saw the holy one among the sainted martyrs of the Land of Israel that was rising to rebirth." Amir Gilboa, "My Three Brenners" [Hebrew], Me'oznaim 32:1 (1971), 53.

25. See the introductory essay by Yitshak Bakon in Yosef Haim Brenner: Mivhar ma'amarei bikoret al yetsirato hasifrutit [Yosef Haim Brenner: A Selection of Critical Essays on his Literary Works], ed. Yitshak Bakon (Tel Aviv, 1972), pp. 7-36; see also Jeffrey Fleck, "Brenner in the Seventies," Prooftexts 3 (1983), 285-294.

26. For a concise "cultural biography" of Agnon, see Band, Nostalgia and Nightmare, pp. 1-28.

27. See, for example, Gershon Shaked's exemplary analysis of the story "Hefker" in his Omanut hasipur shel Agnon, pp. 89-132.

28. Kol kitvei Ahad Ha-Am [The Complete Writings of Ahad Ha-Am] (Tel Aviv, 1965), p. 180; quoted in Shaked, Hasiporet ha'ivrit, p. 53.

29. In an early essay, Belinsky defined narodnost' literature as "...a reflection of the individuality, of the character of a nation, an expression of its inner as well as of its external life, with all of its typical nuances, colors, and birthmarks..." Quoted in Victor Terras, Belinskij and Russian Literary Criticism (Madison, 1974), p. 93. See also René Wellek, A History of Modern Criticism: 1775-1950, IV (New Haven, 1965), 238-265.

30. Isaiah Berlin, Russian Thinkers (New York, 1979), p. 181.

31. V.G. Belinsky, "Thoughts and Notes on Russian Literature" in Belinsky, Chernyshevsky, and Dobrolyubov: Selected Criticism, ed. Ralph E. Matlaw (New York, 1962), pp. 9-11.

32. Kol kitvei Ahad Ha-Am, p. 127; originally published in Hashilo'ah 1 (1896-97), 1-6.

33. Although Belinsky believed that art, by its very nature, was organically linked to social and national issues and, particularly in his last years, wrote passionately of the social responsibility of literature, he also believed in the "autonomy" of art and criticized works which he felt were written simply to argue or illustrate a principle or platform. Belinsky accepted "as granted by nature," comments Victor Terras, "what a utilitarian aesthetic seeks to safeguard by its prescriptions to, and pressures upon, the poet." Terras, Belinskij and Russian Literary Criticism, p. 102.

34. Quoted in Rufus W. Mathewson, Jr., The Positive Hero in Russian Literature, 2nd ed. (Stanford, 1975), p. 27.

35. H.N. Bialik, "Mendele and the Three Volumes" [Hebrew] in Kol kitvei H.N. Bialik, p. 243.

36. See Mathewson, The Positive Hero, pp. 29-30.

37. See Robert A. Maguire, ed. Gogol from the Twentieth Century (Princeton, 1974), pp. 10-11.

38. Ibid., p. 6.

39. See, for example, Y. ben Yeshurun, "The Influence of Russian Prose on Mendele" [Hebrew], Orlogin 7 (1953), 216-219.

40. Quoted in Mathewson, The Positive Hero, p. 40.

41. Quoted in Gershon Shaked, Lelo motsa [No Exit] (Tel Aviv, 1973), p. 67.

42. Kol kitvei Y.H. Brenner [The Complete Writings of Y.H. Brenner], I (Tel Aviv, 1961), 322.

43. For a brief survey of the literature, see Gila Ramras-Rauch, Y.H. Brenner vehasifrut hamodernit [Y.H. Brenner and Modern Literature] (Tel Aviv, 1979), pp. 187-192.

44. H.N. Bialik, "Letter on Beside the Point" [Hebrew], reprinted in Bakon, Mivhar ma'amarim, pp. 45-46.

45. Baruch Kurzweil emphasizes those protagonists' attraction to the Nietzschean figures. See "The Influence of the Philosophy of Life on Hebrew Literature at the Beginning of the Twentieth Century" [Hebrew] in his Sifrutenu hahadasha -- hemshekh o mahapekhah [Our New Literature -- Continuation or Revolution] (Jerusalem, 1960), pp. 250-259.

46. "The Young Agnon -- While in Germany" [Hebrew], Ha'arets, 26, July 1963.

47. Malacahi Bet-Aryeh, "From the Letters of S.Y. Agnon to S.Z. Shocken" [Hebrew] in S.Y. Agnon: Mekharim ute'udot, p. 100.

48. Band, Nostalgia and Nightmare, p. 448.

49. The exchange is related in Alter, "S.Y. Agnon: The Alphabet of Holiness," in his After the Tradition, p. 132.

50. Mathewson, The Positive Hero, p. 14.

51. N.A. Dobrolyubov, "What is Oblomovitis?" in Matlaw, Belinsky, Chernyshevsky, and Dobrolyubov, p. 140.

52. Quoted in James H. Billington, The Icon and the Axe: An Interpretive History of Russian Culture (New York, 1970), p. 387.

53. N.G. Chernyshevsky, "The Russian at the Rendez-vous" in Matlaw, Belinsky, Chernyshevsky, and Dobrolyubov, p. 120.

54. Mathewson, The Positive Hero, p. 3.

55. See, for example, S. Rabinovitsh's (Sholem Aleichem) discussion of the Jewish heroine in "A Letter to a Good Friend" [Yiddish] in Yidishe folks-biblyotek II (1889), 304-310.

56. Shelomo Tsemah, "In the Thrall of Manners" [Hebrew], Me'asef ha'arets (Odessa, 1919), p. 134.

57. See Chapter IV, pp. 61-62.

58. Mathewson, The Positive Hero, pp. 36-37.

59. Kol kitvei Mendele Mokher Sefarim [Complete Writings of Mendele Mokher Sefarim] (Tel Aviv, 1947), p. 259.

60. Mathewson, The Positive Hero, p. 15.

61. Billington, The Icon and the Axe, pp. 331-332.

62. H.Y. Katzenelson, "Conversations on the Matter of Literature" [Hebrew], reprinted in Bakon, Mivhar ma'amarim, 54.

NOTES TO CHAPTER TWO

1. Ian Watt dates the triumph of modern "formal realism" from the works of Defoe, Richardson, and Fielding in which the task of conveying the "impression of fidelity to human experience" took precedence over "conformity to traditional practice" and received standards of "literary decorum." A major element of this new realism was, according to Watt, the presentation of characters as "particular people in particular circumstances," which was achieved, in part, by naming them "in exactly the same way as particular individuals are named in ordinary life." See Ian Watt, The Rise of the Novel (Berkeley, 1965), pp. 13, 18. Working from a much broader perspective, Erich Auerbach traces the fate of realism -- "the serious treatment of everyday reality" -- from the ancient Hebrews and Greeks to the works of Virginia Woolf. Still, like Watt, Auerbach associates the triumph of "modern realism" -- which represents, for Auerbach, a "revolution" against classical and neo-classical doctrines of mimesis and which differed significantly from "medieval realism" -- with the rise of the novel. Auerbach, however, places the scene of that triumph in nineteenth-century France rather than England where, in his view, the break with the past, though initiated earlier, was more gradual and less clear-cut. See Erich Auerbach, Mimesis: The Representation of Reality in Western Literature (Princeton, 1953), pp. 491-492, 554-555.

Notes

2. Marvin Mudrick, "Character and Event in Fiction," Yale Review, No. 2 (Winter 1961), p. 211.

3. Seymour Chatman, Story and Discourse: Narrative Structure in Fiction and Film (Ithaca, 1978), p. 138.

4. What happens, then, when the empirical basis of psychoanalysis is called into question? See, for example, Frederick Crews, "Analysis Terminable," Commentary, July 1980, pp. 25-34.

5. W.J. Harvey, one of the few Anglo-American critics to devote an entire work to these questions, states: "Modern criticism, by and large, has relegated the treatment of character to the periphery of its attention, has at best given it a polite and perfunctory nod and has regarded it more often as a misguided and misleading abstraction. Plenty of 'character sketches' still appear which serve only as easy targets for such hostility." See W.J. Harvey, Character and the Novel (Ithaca, 1965), p. 192.

6. E.M. Forster, Aspects of the Novel (Hardmondsworth, 1962), p. 52.

7. See, for example, Boris Tomashevsky, "Thematics" in Russian Formalist Criticism: Four Essays, ed. Lee T. Lemon and Marion J. Reis (Lincoln, 1965), pp. 78-87.

8. See Piaget's definition of structure in Jean Piaget, Structuralism (New York, 1970), pp. 3-16.

9. Roland Barthes, "Introduction to the Structural Analysis of Narratives," in Image-Music-Text, trans. Stephen Heath (New York, 1977), p. 106.

10. See my discussion of the work of Barthes and Hrushovski, pp. 30-40.

11. Tomashevsky, "Thematics," p. 66ff.

12. See, for example, Jonathan Culler, Structuralist Poetics (Ithaca, 1975), p. 207; Terence Hawkes, Structuralism and Semiotics (Berkeley, 1977), p. 95.

13. V. Propp, Morphology of the Folktale, 2nd ed., trans. Lawrence Scott (Austin, 1968), p. 21.

14. A.J. Greimas, Sémantique Structurale (Paris, 1966), pp. 18-29.

15. Hawkes, Structuralism and Semiotics, p. 90.

16. Ibid., p. 90.

17. Culler, Structuralist Poetics, p. 232.

18. Tzvetan Todorov, Grammaire du Décaméron (The Hague, 1969), p. 18.

19. Todorov, "The Grammar of Narrative," in his The Poetics of Prose, trans. Richard Howard (Ithaca, 1977), pp. 117-118.

20. Todorov, "Narrative-Men," in The Poetics of Prose, p. 66.

21. Barthes, "The Struggle with the Angel," in Image-Music-Text, p. 136.

22. Barthes, ibid., p. 126.

23. Barthes, "Introduction to the Structural Analysis of Narratives," p. 115.

24. Barthes, S/Z, trans. Richard Miller (New York, 1974), pp. 18-20.

25. On the division of the text into "lexias," see Barthes' explanation on pp. 13-14.

26. Benjamin Hrushovski, Segmentation and Motivation in the Text Continuum of Literary Prose, Papers on Poetics and Semiotics (Tel Aviv, 1976), p. 11.

27. Robert Alter, "Mimesis and the Motive for Fiction," TriQuarterly, 42 (Spring 1978), 235.

NOTES TO CHAPTER THREE

1. Kol kitvei Mendele Mokher Sefarim (S.Y. Abramovitsh) [The Complete Writings of Mendele Mokher Sefarim] (Tel Aviv, 1947), p. 103; Ale verkn fun Mendele Moykher Sforim [The Complete Works in Yiddish], (Warsaw, 1919), XI, 50. Sefer hakabtsanim [The Beggars' Book] was originally published in Yiddish as Fishke der Krumer [Fishke the Lame] in 1869 and appeared in a revised and much expanded version in 1888. Like most of his Yiddish works of fiction, Abramovitsh later translated the novel into Hebrew (in the case of The Beggars' Book, the original Hebrew draft of the first eight chapters was prepared by Haim Naham Bialik under Abramovitsh's supervision). The final version of the Hebrew work appeared in 1909. The present study is based upon the Hebrew novel. We will, however, note significant departures from the earlier Yiddish version. Further citations will appear in square brackets, the Hebrew text signified by an "H" and the Yiddish text signified by a "Y." For an English translation (from the Yiddish), see Mendele Mocher Seforim, Fishke the Lame, trans. Gerald Stillman (New York, 1960).

2. Mendele does, however, suffer a similar breakdown in Chapter 5 of "Biymei hara'ash" [In the Days of Fury], Kol kitvei Mendele Mokher Sefarim, pp. 413-414.

3. For Mendele as the "most Jewish of the Jews," see David Frishman, Kol kitvei David Frishman, 2nd ed. (Warsaw, 1938), VI, 70-111; for Mendele as folk-type or archetypical Jew, see the Yiddish critic B. Rivkin, quoted in Dan Miron, A Traveler Disguised (New York, 1973), p. 171; for Mendele's tragic consciousness, see Gershon Shaked, Ben sehok ledema [Between Laughter and Tears], 2nd ed. (Ramat Gan, 1974), p. 68; for Mendele as alienated humanist and apostate, see Miron, A Traveler Disguised, p. 148; for an attack upon Mendele as an anti-semite, see A. Kariv, Adabrah veyirvah li [I Will Speak and Be at Ease] (Tel Aviv, 1950).

4. On the "pseudonym fallacy," see Dan Miron's excellent discussion in A Traveler Disguised, pp. 130-168.

5. Miron, A Traveler Disguised, p. 169.

6. Shaked, Ben sehok ledema, p. 63.

7. Miron, A Traveler Disguised, p. 178.

8. Similar anatomies of Jewish life in the Pale are found on pp. 95, 98, 100, 101, 114, and 122 of the Hebrew text.

9. Reb Alter's consternation is lacking in the Yiddish.

10. On the use of skaz and the foregrounding of the narrative in Gogol, see Boris Eichenbaum, "How Gogol's 'Overcoat' is Made," in Gogol from the Twentieth Century, ed. Robert A. Maguire (Princeton, 1974), pp. 269-291; for a specific comparison between Mendele and Gogol, as well as other Russian writers, see Y. ben Yeshurun, "The Influence of Russian Prose Fiction on Mendele" [Hebrew], Orlogin, 7 (1953), 216-219.

11. The biblical allusion does not appear in the Yiddish. Rather, Reb Alter appears to get "a bit healthier" at the prospect of doing business: "Men zet, vi es kumpt im tsu a shtik gezunt."

Notes

12. The "modified" allusion does not appear in the Yiddish: "Beyde tsdodim hobn dervayl funem gantsn mase-matn keyn groshn in di oygn nisht gezen un geblibn shtark tsufridn, glat fumem handl aleyn."

13. Genesis Rabbah 65:20,21 on Genesis 27:22. The biblical phrases appear in Hebrew in the Yiddish text.

14. The biblical allusions are from Song of Songs 2:16, Gen. 41:2, and Ps. 42:4. They do not appear in the Yiddish text.

15. Yosef Klausner, Yotsrei tekufah umamshikhei tekufah [The Creators of an Age and the Continuers of an Age] (Tel Aviv, 1956), pp. 47-55.

16. Shaked, Ben sehok ledema, p. 65.

17. Miron, A Traveler Disguised, pp. 203-268.

18. Shalom Luria, Halashon hafigurativit bitsirato haduleshonit shel Mendele Mokher Sefarim [Figurative Language in the Bilingual Works of Mendele Mokher Sefarim], Ph.D. diss. The Hebrew University (1977), p. 67.

19. The particular phrase, which has the flavor of a rabbinic aphorism, is lacking in the Yiddish.

20. For the Russian Formalists, the extent to which a novel "bares the device" was often deemed a measure of its artistic excellence. Viktor Shklovsky, for example, declared Tristram Shandy "the most typical novel in world literature" on this basis. See his "Sterne's Tristram Shandy: Stylistic Commentary," in Russian Formalist Criticism: Four Essays, ed. Lemon and Reis (Lincoln, 1965). Roland Barthes recognized, on the other hand, that many writers of fiction, especially the "bourgeois novelists" of the nineteenth century, attempt to conceal artifice. Thus, he distinguishes between "readerly" fiction, that is, fiction that attempts to lull the reader into accepting its conventions as natural, and "writerly" fiction that intentionally subverts conventions in order to reveal the essential artificiality of all narrative. See his Writing Degree Zero and Elements of Semiology, trans. Annette Lavers and Colin Smith (Boston, 1967), pp. 55-61, and S/Z, pp. 3-4. Robert Alter treats some "writerly" texts at length in his Partial Magic: The Novel as a Self-Conscious Genre (Berkely, 1975). Alter identifies a distinct tradition of self-conscious novelists intent upon flaunting narrative artifice stretching from Cervantes to Vladimir Nabokov. That tradition, he notes, fell into eclipse during the nineteenth century, in part because interest shifted from the nature of narrative itself to the pressing historical and social issues of the day.

21. An English translation of the "autobiographical sketch" appears in Mendele Mokher Sefarim, The Parasite, trans. Gerald Stillman (New York, 1956), pp. 19-24.

22. Barthes, S/Z, pp. 67-68.

23. The need for a knowledge of "life" in order to engage in what Barthes calls the process of "nomination" is made clear by his inclusion of a "cultural code" in his treatment of Balzac's "Sarrasine" and particularly by his admission that, ultimately, "all codes are cultural." See S/Z, p. 18.

NOTES TO CHAPTER FOUR

1. Kol kitvei Mendele Mokher Sefarim, p. 259.
2. Kol kitvei Y.H. Brenner, I, 7.
3. Gérard Genette, Narrative Discourse: An Essay in Method (Ithaca, 1979), pp. 212ff.
4. The new emphasis upon the "individualization" of character in Hebrew fiction at the turn of the century is discussed in detail by Shimon Halkin in his Mavo lasiporet ha'ivrit [Introduction to Hebrew Narrative Fiction], ed. Tsofia Hillel (Jerusalem, 1958), pp. 399ff.
5. M.Y. Berdyczweski, "Two Evaluations" [Hebrew], in Bakon, Mivhar ma'amarim, p. 39.
6. H.N. Bialik Igrot Bialik [Bialik's Letters] (Tel Aviv, 1931) I, 268-270; reprinted in Bakon, Mivhar ma'amarim, pp. 45-46.
7. Quoted in Bakon, Mivhar ma'amarim, p. 16.
8. Ibid., p. 21.
9. H.Y. Katzenelson, "Conversations on the Matter of Literature" [Hebrew], in Bakon, Mivhar ma'amarim, p. 54.
10. Ba'al Mahshavot, "Around the Point" [Hebrew], in Bakon, Mivhar ma'amarim, p. 61.
11. Halkin, Mavo lasiporet ha'ivrit, p. 334.
12. Quoted in Bakon, Mivhar ma'amarim, p. 17.
13. Baruch Kurzweil, Ben hazon leven ha'absurdi [Between Vision and the Absurd] (Tel Avid, 1973), p. 274.
14. Leon Edel, The Modern Psychological Novel (New York, 1964), pp. 11-26.
15. Y.H. Brenner, "The Land of Israel Genre and Its Trappings" [Hebrew], in Kol kitvei Y.H. Brenner, II, 269-270.
16. See, for example, Dorrit Cohn, Transparent Minds: Narrative Modes for Presenting Consciousness in Fiction (Princeton, 1978), pp. 21-140.
17. Gershon Shaked, "Before the Throne of Judgment" [Hebrew] in his Lelo motsa [No Exit], pp. 79-98; Yosef Ewen, Omanut hasipur shel Y.H. Brenner [The Narrative Craft of Y.H. Brenner] (Jerusalem, 1977), pp. 175-195.
18. Bertril Romberg, Studies in the Narrative Techniques of the First-Person Novel (Stockholm, 1962).
19. "The tone of autobiography tends to be ironic or comic, because it usually represents experience gazing backward at the innocent illusions of the child that fathered the man and because it reflects the individual's ability to rise above circumstances, if only through retrospective analysis." Stephen Shapiro, "The Dark Continent of Literature: Autobiography," Comparative Literature Studies, 5, No. 4 (December 1968), 447. See also Roy Pascal, Design and Truth in Autobiography (Cambridge: Harvard University Press, 1960).

20. Kol kitvei Y.H. Brenner I, 25. All further references to In Winter appear in the text. All translations are my own.

21. Genette, Narrative Discourse, pp. 256-257.

22. Dan Miron, "On the Problems of Y.H. Brenner's Style" [Hebrew] in his Kivvun orot [Back to Focus] (Jerusalem, 1979), pp. 357-68. The essay was originally published in Gazit 19:9-12 (1961), 50-54.

23. Dorrit Cohn, Transparent Minds, pp. 99ff.

24. Dov Sadan, "Chapters on the Psychology of Y.H. Brenner" [Hebrew] Ahdut ha'avodah 3:1-2 (1931), 103-116; reprinted in Bakon, Mivhar ma'amarim, pp. 113-132.

25. See, for example, Shaked, hasiporet ha'ivrit, pp.375-376.

NOTES TO CHAPTER FIVE

1. Shaked, "Art of Authenticity" (Hebrew), in his Lelo motsa, pp. 66-78.

2. Joseph Chaim Brenner, Breakdown and Bereavement, trans. Hillel Halkin (Ithaca, 1971), p. 11. All further references to this work appear in the text. Halkin's translation has, in places, been revised.

3. Cohn, Transparent Minds, p. 99ff.

4. Mikhail Bakhtin, "Discourse Typology in Prose," in Readings in Russian Poetics: Formalist and Structuralist Views, ed. Ladislav Matejka and Krystyna Pomorska (Cambridge, 1971), pp. 176-196.

5. See Yosef Ewen, "Indirect Monologue: A Concept in the Theory of Prose and its Manifestations in Hebrew Narrative Fiction" [Hebrew], 1:1 (1968), 140-152; see also Ewen's Omanut hasipur shel Y.H. Brenner, pp. 141-153.

6. Lionel Trilling, "The Fate of Pleasure," in his Beyond Culture (New York, 1968), pp. 57-88.

7. F. Lahover, "Y.H. Brenner" [Hebrew], in Bakon, Mivhar ma'amarim, p. 81.

8. Natan Zach, "Sickness and the Hidden Sweetness" [Hebrew], Amot 1:2 (1962), 40-46; reprinted in Bakon, Mivhar ma'amarim, pp. 197-198.

9. Fyodor Dostoyevsky, Notes from Underground, trans. Andrew R. MacAndrew (New York, 1961), p. 203.

NOTES TO CHAPTER SIX

1. Kol sipurav shel Shemuel Yosef Agnon [Complete Stories of Shemuel Yosef Agnon], V (Jerusalem, 1971), 223. All further references to this work appear in the text. All translations are my own.

2. Robert Alter analyzes the allusions to traditional sources in the opening passage of Only Yesterday in After the Tradition, pp. 197-201.

3. Band, Nostalgia and Nightmare, p. 419.

4. Baruch Kurzweil, Masot 'al sipure Shai Agnon [Essays on the Stories of Shai Agnon] (Tel Aviv, 1970), pp. 95-115.

5. Baruch Hochman, The Fiction of S.Y. Agnon (Ithaca, 1970), pp. 140-141.

6. Meshulam Tokhner, Pesher Agnon [Cipher to Agnon] (Tel Aviv, 1968), pp. 69-79.

7. "If a parallel exists between man and dog, it is the latter's role that is decisive, and if their fates reflect upon each other, it is not the dog who is the animal-like reflection of Yitshak, but rather Yitshak is the human reflection of the dog... He [Balak] reveals the ridiculous but real canine farce that lies beneath the melancholy aspect of the human drama." Eli Shvaid, Shalosh ashmarot [Three Watches of the Night] (Tel Aviv, 1964), p. 50.

8. Shaked, Omanut hasipur shel Agnon, pp. 47-64.

9. Heinz Politzer, Franz Kafka: Parable and Paradox (Ithaca, 1966), p. 90.

10. Franz Kafka, Selected Short Stories of Franz Kafka, trans. Willa and Edwin Muir (New York, 1952), p. 172.

11. Ibid., p. 225.

12. Ibid., p. 215.

13. The term "bisociation" is used by Arthur Koestler to describe the "clash between two mutually incompatible codes, or associate contexts" which is, for him, the fundamental mechanism of humor. Because they behave as if they were human without losing their animal appearance, the animal-creatures of fable "live on the line of intersection of the two planes." See his The Act of Creation (New York, 1964), pp. 35, 67.

14. Victor Erlich, Russian Formalism: History-Doctrine (New Haven, 1965), p. 258.

15. "...within the parabolic framework of the novel K.'s guilt acquires the mysterious air of complete impenetrability. Remaining to the last undefined, it appears also all-encompassing, just as K., by remaining a nondescript Everyman, appears as a universal type." Politzer, Parable and Paradox, p. 177. For this reason, Politzer holds that the main subject of Kafka's novel is not the "paradox of K.'s guilt" but the "much more vexing paradox of the Law that violated itself by his arrest."

NOTES TO CHAPTER SEVEN

1. Roland Barthes, "Introduction to the Structural Analysis of Narratives," in his Image-Music-Text, trans. Stephen Heath (New York, 1977), p. 93.

2. Tzvetan Todorov, "Narrative-Men," in his The Poetics of Prose, trans. Richard Howard (Ithaca, 1977), pp. 68-69.

3. Kol kitve Y.H. Brenner, I, 25.

4. Michel Foucault makes this point with uncharacteristic clarity in "The Discourse on Language," in his The Archaeology of Knowledge, trans. A.M. Sheridan Smith (New York, 1972), pp. 215-237.

WORKS CONSULTED

Modern Hebrew Literature, General

Ahad Ha-Am. Kol kitvei Ahad Ha-Am [The Complete Writings of Ahad Ha-am]. Tel Aviv, 1965.

Alter, Robert. After the Tradition: Essays on Modern Jewish Writing. New York, 1971.

Bialik, H.N. Kol kitvei H.N. Bialik [The Complete Writings of H.N. Bialik]. Tel Aviv, 1965.

Feierberg, M.Z. Whither? and Other Stories. Trans. Hillel Halkin. Philadelphia, 1973.

Halkin, Shimon. Mavo lasiporet ha'ivrit: Reshimot lefi hartsa'otav shel Professor S. Halkin [Introduction to Hebrew Narrative Prose: Notes According to the Lectures of Professor S. Halkin]. Jerusalem, 1958.

Klausner, Yosef. Historiah shel hasifrut ha'ivrit [A History of Hebrew Literature]. 8 vols. Jerusalem, 1949-1953.

-------. Yotsrei tekufah unmamshikhei tekufah [The Creators of an Age and the Continuers of an Age]. Tel Aviv, 1956.

Kurzweil, Baruch. Ben hazon leven ha'absurdi [Between Vision and the Absurd]. Jerusalem, 1966.

-------. Sifrutenu hahadasha -- hemshekh o mahapekha [Our New Literature -- Continuation or Revolution]. Jerusalem, 1965.

Lahover, Fishel. Toldot hasifrut ha'ivrit hahadasha [The History of Modern Hebrew Literature]. 2 vols. Tel Aviv, 1967.

Miron, Dan. "Hebrew Literature at the Beginning of the Twentieth Century" [Hebrew]. Me'asef agudat hasofrim, 2 (1961), 436-464.

Patterson, David. Abraham Mapu: The Creator of the Modern Hebrew Novel. London, 1964.

-------. The Hebrew Novel in Czarist Russia. Edinburgh, 1964.

Rabinovich, Isaiah. Hasiporet ha'ivrit mehapeset gibor [Hebrew Fiction in Search of a Hero]. Tel Aviv, 1967.

Sadan, Dov. Avnei Bedek [Touchstones]. Tel Aviv, 1963.

-------. Ben din leheshbon: Masot 'al sofrim usefarim [Between Judgment and Account: Essays on Writers and Books]. Tel Aviv, 1963.

Sha'anan, A. Hasifrut ha'ivrit hahadasha lizerameha [Trends in Modern Hebrew Literature]. 5 vols. Tel Aviv, 1962-1978.

Shaked, Gershon. Hasiporet ha'ivrit: 1880-1970 [Hebrew Narrative Fiction: 1880-1978]. Vol. I. Jerusalem, 1978.

S.Y. Abramovitsh

Works

Ale Verkn fun Mendele Moykher-Sforim [The Complete Works in Yiddish]. 17 vols. Warsaw, 1910.

Kol kitvei Mendele Mokher Sefarim [The Complete Writings of Mendele Mokher Serarim]. Tel Aviv, 1947.

Fishke the Lame. Trans. Gerald Stillman. New York, 1960.

The Parasite. Trans. Gerald Stillman. New York, 1956.

Criticism

Bialik, H.N. "Mendele ushloshet hakerakhim" [Hebrew]. In Kol kitvei H.N. Bialik [The Complete Writings of H.N. Bialik]. Tel Aviv, 1965.

Brenner, Y.H. "Ha'arakhat 'atsmenu bishloshet hakerakhim" [Hebrew]. In Kol kitvei Y.H. Brenner [The Complete Writings of Y.H. Brenner]. Vol. 3. Tel Aviv, 1967.

Kariv, Avraham. Adabra veyirvah li [I Will Speak and Be at Ease]. Tel Aviv, 1951.

Luria, Shalom. Halashon hafigurativit bitsirato hadulashonit shel Mendele Mokher Sefarim [Figurative Language in the Bilingual Works of Mendele Mokher Sefarim]. Ph.D. diss. The Hebrew University, 1977.

Miron, Dan. "Fishke hahigar me'et Shai Abramovitsh" [Hebrew]. Hasifrut, 17 (1974), 92-126.

-------. A Traveler Disguised: The Rise of Modern Yiddish Fiction in the Nineteenth Century. New York, 1973.

Peri, Menachem. "Ha'anologia umekoma bemivneh haroman shel Mendele Mokher Sefarim" [Hebrew]. Hasifrut, 1:1 (1968), 65-100.

Shaked, Gershon. Ben sehok ledema [Between Laughter and Tears]. 2nd ed. Ramat Gan, 1974.

Tsemah, Shelomo. "In the Thrall of Manners" [Hebrew]. Me'asef ha'arets, 1919, 127-148.

Yeshurun, U. ben. "The Influence of Russian Prose on Mendele" [Hebrew]. Orlogin, 7 (1953), 216-219.

Yosef Haim Brenner

Works

Breakdown and Bereavement. Trans. Hillel Halkin. Ithaca, 1971.

Kol kitvei Y.H. Brenner [The Complete Writings of Y.H. Brenner]. 3 vols. Tel Aviv, 1956-1967.

Criticism

Agnon, S.Y. "Y.H. Brenner in Life and Death" [Hebrew]. In Me'atsmi le'atsmi [From Me to Myself]. Jerusalem, 1976.

Bakon, Yitshak. Brenner hatsa'ir: Hayav viytsirotav shel Brenner 'ad lehofa'at "Hame'orer" beLondon [Young Brenner: Brenner's Life and Works up to the Publication of "Hame'orer" in London]. 2 vols. Tel Aviv, 1975.

-------. "Brenner on S.Y. Agnon" [Hebrew]. Me'oznaim, 27:3-4 (1968), 210-216.

-------, ed. Yosef Haim Brenner: Mivhar ma'amere bikoret 'al yetsirato hasifrutit [Yosef Haim Brenner: A Selection of Critical Essays on His Literary Works]. Tel Aviv, 1972.

Cutter, William, and Ewen, Yosef, "Following Brenner on the Road to Breakdown and Bereavement" [Hebrew]. Hasifrut, 17 (1974), 127-144.

Ewen, Yosef. "Indirect Monologue: A Concept in the Theory of Prose and its Manifestations in Hebrew Narrative Fiction" [Hebrew]. Hasifrut, 1:1 (1968), 140-152.

-------. Omanut hasipur shel Y.H. Brenner [Y.H. Brenner's Narrative Craft]. Jerusalem, 1977.

Fleck, Jeffrey. "Brenner in the Seventies." Prooftexts 3 (1983), 285-294.

Gilboa, Amir. "My Three Brenners" [Hebrew]. Me'oznaim 32:1 (1971), 58-9.

Kurzweil, Baruch. "The Influence of the Philosophy of Life on Hebrew Literature at the Beginning of the 20th Century" [Hebrew]. In Sifrutenu hahadasha -- hemshekh o mahapekha [Our New Literature -- Continuation or Revolution]. Jerusalem, 1960.

-------. "The Meaning of Suffering and Life in the Stories of Y.H. Brenner" [Hebrew]. In Ben hazon leven ha'absurdi [Between Vision and the Absurd]. Jerusalem, 1966.

Ramras-Rauch, Gila. Y.H. Brenner vehasifrut hamodernit [Y.H. Brenner and Modern Literature]. Tel Aviv, 1979.

Shaked, Gershon, Lelo motsa [No Exit]. Tel Aviv, 1973.

Snir, M., ed. Yosef Haim Brenner: Mivhar zikhronot [Yosef Haim Brenner: A Selection of Memoirs]. Tel Aviv, 1971.

Werses, Shemuel. "Between Brenner and Mendele" [Hebrew]. Mahbarot leheker yetsirato ufe'ulo shel Y.H. Brenner. Ed. Yisrael Levin. Tel Aviv, 1975.

S.Y. Agnon

Works

Kol sipurav shel Shemuel Yosef Agnon [The Complete Stories of Shemuel Yosef Agnon]. 8 vols. Tel Aviv, 1971.

Criticism

Bakon, Yitshak. "On the Year of Agnon's Aliyah and its Implications" [Hebrew]. Hapo'el hatsa'ir 39:27-28 (April 1968), 23-25.

Band, Arnold J. Nostalgia and Nightmare: A Study in the Fiction of S.Y. Agnon. Berkeley, 1968.

Barzel, Hillel, ed. Shemuel Yosef Agnon: Mivhar ma'amarim 'al yetsirato [Shemuel Yosef Agnon: A Selection of Essays on His Work]. Tel Aviv, 1982.

Hochman, Baruch. The Fiction of S.Y. Agnon. Ithaca, 1970.

Kurzweil, Baruch. Masot 'al sipure Shai Agnon [Essays on the Stories of Shai Agnon]. Tel Aviv, 1970.

Shaked, Gershon. Omanut hasipur shel Agnon [The Narrative Art of S.Y. Agnon]. Merhavia, 1973.

Shaked, G. and Weiser, R., ed. S.Y. Agnon: Mekharim ute'udot [S.Y. Agnon: Studies and Documents]. Jerusalem, 1978.

Shvaid, Eli. Shalosh ashmorot [Three Watches of the Night]. Tel Aviv, 1964.

Tokhner, Meshulam. Pesher Agnon [Cipher to Agnon]. Tel Aviv, 1968.

"The Young Agnon -- While in Germany" [Hebrew]. Ha'arets 26 (July 1963).

Theory, Criticism, Background

Alter, Robert. "Mimesis and the Motive for Fiction." TriQuarterly 42 (Spring 1978), 228-248.

--------. Partial Magic: The Novel as a Self-Conscious Genre. Berkeley, 1975.

Auerbach, Erich. Mimesis: The Representation of Reality in Western Literature. Princeton, 1953.

Barthes, Roland. Image-Music-Text. Trans. Stephen Heath. New York, 1977.

--------. S/Z. Trans. Richard Miller. New York, 1974.

--------. Writing Degree Zero and Elements of Semiology. Trans. Annette Lavers and Colin Smith. Boston, 1967.

Berlin, Isaiah. Russian Thinkers. Ed. Henry Hardy and Aileen Kelly. New York, 1979.

Billington, James H. The Icon and the Axe: An Interpretive History of Russian Culture. New York, 1970.

Chatman, Seymour. Story and Discourse: Narrative Structure in Fiction and Film. Ithaca, 1978.

Cohn, Dorrit. Transparent Minds: Narrative Modes for Presenting Consciousness in Fiction. Princeton, 1978.

Crews, Frederick. "Analysis Terminable." Commentary (July 1980), pp. 25-34.

Culler, Jonathan. Structuralist Poetics: Structuralism, Linguistics and the Study of Literature. Ithaca, 1975.

Dostoyevsky, Fyodor. Notes from Underground. Trans. Andrew R. MacAndrew. New York, 1961.

Edel, Leon. The Modern Psychological Novel. New York, 1964.

Eichenbaum, Boris. "How Gogol's 'Overcoat' Is Made." In Gogol from the Twentieth Century. Ed. and trans. Robert A. Maguire. Princeton, 1974.

Erlich, Victor. Russian Formalism: History-Doctrine. 3rd edition. New Haven, 1965.

Forster, E.M. Aspects of the Novel. Harmondsworth, 1962.

Foucault, Michel. The Archaeology of Knowledge. New York, 1972.

Freud, Sigmund. The Interpretation of Dreams. Trans. James Strachey. New York, 1965.

-------. Jokes and Their Relation to the Unconscious. Trans. James Strachey. New York, 1960.

Genette, Gérard. Narrative Discourse: An Essay in Method. Trans. Jane E. Lewin. Ithaca, 1980.

Gogol, Nikolai. Dead Souls. Trans. Andrew R. MacAndrew. New York, 1961.

-------. The Diary of a Madman and Other Stories. Trans. Andrew R. MacAndrew. New York, 1960.

Greimas, A.J. Sémantique Structurale. Paris, 1966.

Harvey, W.J. Character and the Novel. Ithaca, 1965.

Hawkes, Terence. Structuralism and Semiotics. Berkeley, 1977.

Hrushovski, Benjamin. "Segmentation and Motivation in the Text Continuum of Literary Prose: The First Episode of War and Peace." Papers on Poetics and Semiotics, 5. Tel Aviv, 1976.

Jameson, Fredric. The Prison House of Language. Princeton, 1972.

Kafka, Franz. Selected Stories. Trans. Willa and Edwin Muir. New York, 1952.

-------. The Trial. Trans. Willa and Edwin Muir. Rev. E.M. Butler. New York, 1964.

Koestler, Arthur. The Act of Creation. New York, 1964.

Lemon, Lee T. and Marion J. Reis, eds. Russian Formalist Criticism: Four Essays. Lincoln, 1965.

Maguire, Robert A., ed. Gogol from the Twentieth Century: Eleven Essays. Princeton, 1974.

Matejka, Ladislav and Krystyna Pomorska, eds. Readings in Russian Poetics: Formalist and Structuralist Views. Cambridge, 1971.

Mathewson, Rufus W., Jr. The Positive Hero in Russian Literature. 2nd ed. Stanford, 1975.

Matlaw, Ralph E., ed. Belinsky, Chernyshevsky, and Dobrolyubov: Selected Criticism. New York, 1962.

Mirsky, D.S. A History of Russian Literature: From its Beginnings to 1900. New York, 1958.

Mudrick, Marvin. "Character and Event in Fiction." Yale Review (Winter 1961), 202-218.

Pascal, Roy. Design and Truth in Autobiography. Cambridge, 1960.

Piaget, Jean. Structuralism. New York, 1970.

Politzer, Heinz. Franz Kafka: Parable and Paradox. Ithaca, 1966.

Price, Martin. "The Other Self: Thoughts about Character in the Novel." In Imagined Worlds: Essays... in Honour of John Butt. Ed. M. Mack. London, 1968.

Propp, V. Morphology of the Folktale. 2nd ed. Trans. Lawrence Scott. Austin, 1968.

Rabinovitsh, S. (Sholem Aleichem). "A Letter to a Good Friend" [Yiddish]. Yidishe folks-biblyotek, II (1889), 304-310.

Romberg, Bertril. Studies in the Narrative Technique of the First-Person Novel. Stockholm, 1962.

Scholes, Robert and Robert Kellog. The Nature of Narrative. London, 1966.

Shapiro, Stephen. "The Dark Continent of Literature: Autobiography." Comparative Literature Studies 5, No. 4 (December 1968), 440-456.

Terras, Victor. Belinskij and Russian Literary Criticism. Madison, 1974.

Todorov, Tzvetan. Grammaire du Décaméron. The Hague, 1969.

-------. The Poetics of Prose. Trans. Richard Howard. Ithaca, 1977.

Trilling, Lionel. Beyond Culture. New York, 1968.

Watt, Ian. The Rise of the Novel. Berkeley, 1965.

Wellek, René. A History of Modern Criticism: 1750-1950. 5 vols. New Haven, 1965.

Wimsatt, William K. and Cleanth Brooks. Literary Criticism: A Short History. New York, 1957.

Winston, Mathew. "Humour Noir and Black Humor." In Veins of Humor. Ed. Harry Levin. Cambridge, 1972.

INDEX

Abramovitsh, S.Y. (Mendele Mokher Sefarim)
1, 6-13, 15, 17, 19, 20, 43-57, 60-63, 73, 87, 102, 103, 105, 107
The Beggars' Book
6, 43, 45, 46, 49-52, 60, 73, 87, 102, 105
Fathers and Sons
9, 18
In Those Days
19
"Jubilee Edition"
6, 7, 10
"A Letter on Education"
9
Natural History
9
"The Secret Place of Thunder"
10
Agnon, S.Y.
1, 6-9, 12, 13, 17, 20, 87, 88, 92, 93, 95-99, 102, 106-108
"Agunot"
7, 12
"The Banished One"
7
The Book of Deeds
13, 17
"And the Crooked Shall Become Straight"
7
A Guest for the Night
13, 98
"The Hill of Sand"
7
"The Legend of the Scribe"
7
"Legends"
7
"Miriam's Well"
8, 78
Only Yesterday
8, 20, 87, 92-94, 96, 98, 101, 102, 106
Shira
12
Ahad Ha-Am
6, 10, 13-16, 61
Alter, Robert
2, 40, 43, 45-49, 54, 56, 89, 92, 94
Arabian Nights
29, 30
Ba'al Mahshavot
62
Bakhtin, Mikhail
75

Balzac, Honoré de
17, 30, 31, 34
"Sarrasine"
30-37
Band, Arnold
17, 45, 54, 92
Barthes, Roland
1, 24, 30-40, 87, 103-105
"Introduction to the Structural Analysis of Narratives"
24, 27-31, 37, 38, 40, 41, 103, 104
S/Z
30, 37, 40
Belinsky, V.G.
11, 14-16, 19
Ben-Avigdor
6
Berdyczweski, M.Y.
61, 93
Berkovitz, Y.D.
62
Berlin, Isaiah
14
Bershadski, Y.
62
Bialik, H.N.
6, 10, 15, 16, 61
Braudes, Reuben Asher
4
Brenner, Y.H.
1, 6-13, 15-17, 19, 20, 59-64, 67, 69, 70, 72-75, 77, 83, 87, 92, 93, 99, 102, 105-107
Beside the Point
7, 62, 99
Between Water and Water
7
Breakdown and Bereavement
7, 17, 64, 73-75, 79, 82-85
From Here and There
7, 16, 63
From the Valley of Trouble
11
One Year
7
"Self Evaluation in the Three Volumes"
7, 83
In Winter
7, 11, 16, 20, 59-62, 64, 65, 71-73, 82, 85, 99
Chatman, Seymour
22
Chernyshevsky, N.G.
18

Cohn, Dorrit
  69, 75, 76
Culler, Jonathan
  29
Decameron
  29
Dictionary of Philosophy
  22
Dobrolyubov, N.A.
  14, 18, 19
Dostoyevsky, Fyodor
  11, 16, 17, 19, 83
  Crime and Punishment
    11
  Notes from Underground
    19
Edel, Leon
  63
Erlich, Victor
  98
Ewen, Yosef
  64, 65
Feierberg, M.Z.
  6, 62
  Whither
    6
Flaubert, Gustave
  17
Forster, E.M.
  22-24, 31, 32, 34, 36, 41, 105
  Aspects of the Novel
    22
Frishman, David
  6
Genette, Gérard
  60, 65
Gnessin, U.N.
  6, 8, 11, 15, 16, 62, 75
Gogol, Nikolai
  14, 15, 19, 47, 50
  Dead Souls
    15
Goncharov, Ivan
  18
  Oblomov
    18
Gorky, Maxim
  16
Gottlober, A.B.
  9
Greimas, A.J.
  27-29
Halkin, Shimon
  62
Hame'orer
  8
Ha'omer
  7
Hapo'el Hatsa'ir
  7
Hashilo'ah
  14, 16

Haskalah
  3-5, 9-11, 13, 14, 63
Hawkes, Terence
  28
Hochman, Baruch
  94, 95, 106, 107
Hrushovski, Benjamin
  1, 2, 37-40, 87, 104
James, Henry
  29, 30, 63
Joyce, James
  63
Jung, Carl G.
  94
Kafka, Franz
  17, 97, 100
  "Investigations of a Dog"
    97
  "A Report to an Academy"
    97
  The Trial
    100
Kariv, Avraham
  107
Katzenelson, H.Y.
  20, 62
King Lear
  28
Kurzweil, Baruch
  47, 63, 94, 95, 106, 107
Lahover, F.
  63, 83
Lermontov, Mikhail
  18
Lubitzki, Y.A.
  62
Luria, Shalom
  50, 51
Luzzato, Moshe Haim
  4
Mapu, Abraham
  4, 5, 9
  The Hypocrite
    5
  The Love of Zion
    4, 9
Mathewson, Rufus W., Jr.
  17-19
Miron, Dan
  44, 45, 50, 51, 66
Moriah
  6
Mudrick, Marvin
  21, 22
Nietzsche, Friedrich
  16, 77
Odyssey
  29
Orlov
  8
Peretz, Y.L.
  4, 6

Pisarev, D.I.
  16, 18
Propp, Vladimir
  26-29
  <u>Morphology of the Russian Folktale</u>
    26
Proust, Marcel
  63
Pushkin, Alexander
  15, 18
  <u>Eugene Onegin</u>
    18
Rabinovich, Isaiah
  107
Rawnitzki, Y.H.
  6
<u>Revivim</u>
  8
Rolland, Romain
  17
Romberg, Bertril
  64, 65
Rousseau, Jean-Jacques
  65
  <u>Confessions</u>
    65
Russian Formalists
  1, 23, 25, 26, 39, 98, 103
Sadan, Dov
  70
<u>Saragossa Manuscript</u>
  29
Schocken, Salmon
  17
Shaked, Gershon
  10, 11, 13, 15, 44, 64, 65, 96
  <u>Between Laughter and Tears</u>
    10, 15
Shamir, Moshe
  5
  <u>King of Flesh and Blood</u>
    5
Shofman, Gershon
  6, 8, 62

Shvaid, Eli
  95
Smolenskin, Peretz
  4
Strindberg, August
  17
Structuralism
  24, 25
<u>Talush</u>
  19, 20, 62, 63, 93, 97-99, 102
Tchernichowsky, Shaul
  6
Todorov, Tzvetan
  29, 30, 40, 61, 103
Tokhner, Meshulam
  95, 108
  <u>Cipher to Agnon</u>
    95
Tolstoy, Leo
  16, 18
Tomashevsky, Boris
  25-27
  "Thematics"
    25
Trilling, Lionel
  82
Tsemah, Shelomo
  19, 62, 107
Turgenev, Ivan
  18, 19
  "Asya"
    18
  "Diary of a Superfluous Man"
    19
  <u>Fathers and Sons</u>
    9, 18
Woolf, Virginia
  63
Yehoshua, A.B.
  13
Zach, Natan
  83

2124
14